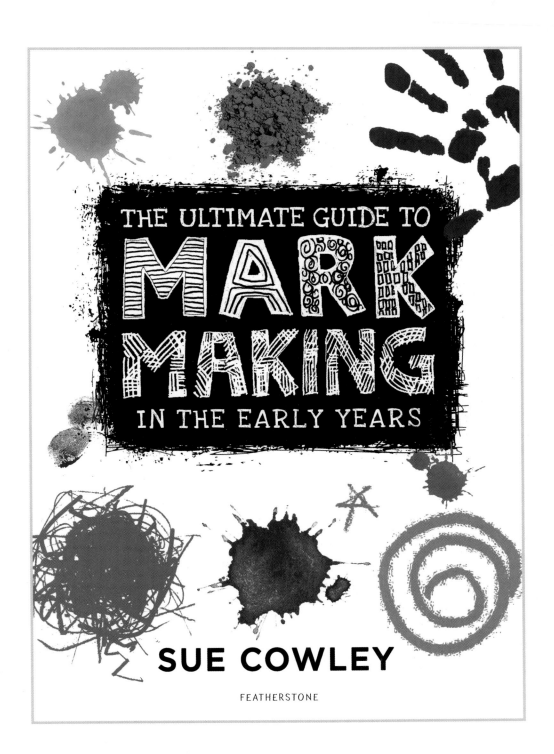

THE ULTIMATE GUIDE TO
MARK MAKING
IN THE EARLY YEARS

SUE COWLEY

FEATHERSTONE

FEATHERSTONE
Bloomsbury Publishing Plc
50 Bedford Square, London, WC1B 3DP, UK

BLOOMSBURY, FEATHERSTONE and the Feather logo are trademarks of Bloomsbury Publishing Plc

First published in Great Britain, 2019 by Bloomsbury Publishing Plc

A catalogue record for this book is available from the British Library

ISBN: PB: 978-1-4729-6708-4; ePDF: 978-1-4729-6707-7; ePub: 978-1-4729-6706-0

2 4 6 8 10 9 7 5 3 1

Text design by Lynda Murray

Printed in China by Leo Paper Products, Heshan, Guangdong

Acknowledgments

Many thanks to all the staff, children, parents and committee members at Stanton Drew and Pensford Preschool, both past and present. It's been a privilege and a pleasure helping to run our setting. Thanks also to all the staff, children and parents who have supported and worked with me in the 'Magazine Team' at Stanton Drew Primary School.

A huge 'thank you' goes to my photographer Manda Le Pivert for her wonderful images of the children playing, learning and making marks. My gratitude must also go to everyone at my publishers Continuum (now Bloomsbury), especially to my editor Melanie Wilson and her assistant Rosie Pattinson. A special vote of thanks as always goes to my family, who support me and who make it possible for me to write.

And finally, thanks particularly to all those children who are featured in the photographs in this book and whose writing I've used: Álvie and Edite Castellino, Jack and Niamh Bishop, Alex Bradbury, Matty Croucher and Shay O'Malley.

This book is dedicated to Lynne Willmott for her commitment to our preschool, and the children who attend it.

Contents

Introduction

A journey of a thousand miles begins with a single step.
Laozi (translated)

It's amazing to think that it only takes about 6 or 7 years from the moment a baby is born to when that same child is typically able to read and write fairly fluently. In that very short space of time, children acquire an entire spoken language (including a subconscious understanding of its grammatical rules). They learn how, when and why we use words to communicate. They develop the physical skills needed to support their bodies and to hold and manipulate a writing tool. They understand how to match spoken sounds with written letters and words, and how different kinds of texts work. And they become confident and motivated enough to put their own words down on the page. When you stop to think about it, it's an incredible achievement, testament to the hard work of the educators and parents who help them develop.

Learning to write, and to write well, is crucial to a child's chances of educational success. Writing is there, right at the heart of pretty much every subject taught within schools. It's something that children must do, each and every day. And if they *can't* do it, if they *can't* access and use language, it's likely that they will become disaffected and begin to misbehave. During my teaching career I've taught children from the age of two, right through to the age of 18. I've seen young children who already have a secure grasp of the written word, but equally I've worked with secondary school students who simply cannot, or will not, write. Something went wrong for them during the earliest years. For some reason, they stumbled while learning the process of writing, and no one was able to get them back on track. Whether you're a nursery or Reception teacher, an early years professional, teacher or practitioner, a nursery nurse, a preschool leader or assistant, a teaching assistant or a childminder, this book is for you. Because whatever your role within the phase is, you are hugely important in setting the child/children in your care off on the right course.

This book is designed to guide you and your children towards the goal of becoming writers. From the very early marks to the thrill of those first proper words and sentences, I give you all the key information you need about the process of learning to write. You will learn about the skills, attributes, attitudes, concepts and knowledge that you must help your children develop or grasp. I will encourage you to have confidence in the approaches that you use, showing you how to boost your children's motivation to make marks, and helping you to inspire *all* your children to become lifelong writers. Although theory is of great value, this book is very much rooted in the practicalities of working with young children.

The journey to becoming a writer can be a tough one, scattered with potential obstacles, particularly for those children who have special educational needs and disabilities. Each child is a unique individual, and the pathway will be different for each one. Some children will skip quickly along, hardly stumbling, picking up the skills required without any trouble at all. For these children, success breeds success, confidence feeds on confidence, attainment comes with ease. Other children struggle, finding it hard to acquire the skills or the motivation to succeed, perhaps because of a specific learning, emotional or behavioural issue, or difficulties at home. Some children will encounter problems with one area of the skill of writing in particular, while others will struggle to make any progress at all. In this book you will find ideas to help *all* your children take the steps needed to become writers.

Learning how to write can, should, indeed *must* be a joyous and exciting journey – writing is not a dull, dry craft, but a vibrant, exciting act of communication. This book shows you how to take your children on the most interactive, multisensory, adventurous, inspirational and dramatic route possible. Yes, there are risks along the way, and things may get messy, but that's the nature of working in the early years. Yes, skills and self-discipline are crucial, but without engagement and motivation, they are of little value. In this book you will find loads of practical activities to help your young mark makers develop into confident, fluent writers, able to express themselves through the written word. Where you see an icon like this, you'll find detailed information about some activities that you can try out in your setting. Wherever you work, the ideas in this book are ones you can use, straight away – today!

activity

Please note that this book is not about getting children to 'meet targets'; nor is it about how to please Ofsted inspectors, local authority advisers or the DfE. It certainly isn't a highly structured set of guidelines for teaching writing that insist the process can only work in one way. Rather, this book is a repository of good ideas, good practice and inspirational activities drawn from my own experiences, observations and from a wide range of professional sources. It's a book about all the great things that early years teachers, practitioners and childminders do every day in their home, preschool, nursery and school settings, that might work for the children in yours. If I have one hope for how this book will work for you, it is that it will help you to trust in your professional judgement, in your gut instinct about what works: that you are encouraged to believe that *you* know what is right for *your* children, because you are the one who works with them every day.

website You will find a range of useful additional resources in the companion website for this book (www.bloomsbury.com/ultimate-mark-making-EY) – case studies that show you how different children might take different routes down the road to writing and downloadable checklists to use when auditing the current provision in your setting. Keep an eye out for the symbol throughout this guide, to discover what other useful materials are on the companion site.

I'd like to finish by wishing you and your children all the best of luck on your journey. As educators, we are hugely fortunate to be able to help our children achieve the gift of becoming writers. It's a gift that allows them to express themselves, their ideas, their opinions, their creativity, through the medium of language. It's a gift that my own teachers gave to me, many years ago, and which allows me to make my living as an author, and to communicate with you right now. To have the chance to make such a difference in a child's life is, to my mind, nothing short of miraculous. Go forth, and perform magic!

Sue Cowley

www.suecowley.co.uk
www.celebrate-writing.co.uk

Starting points

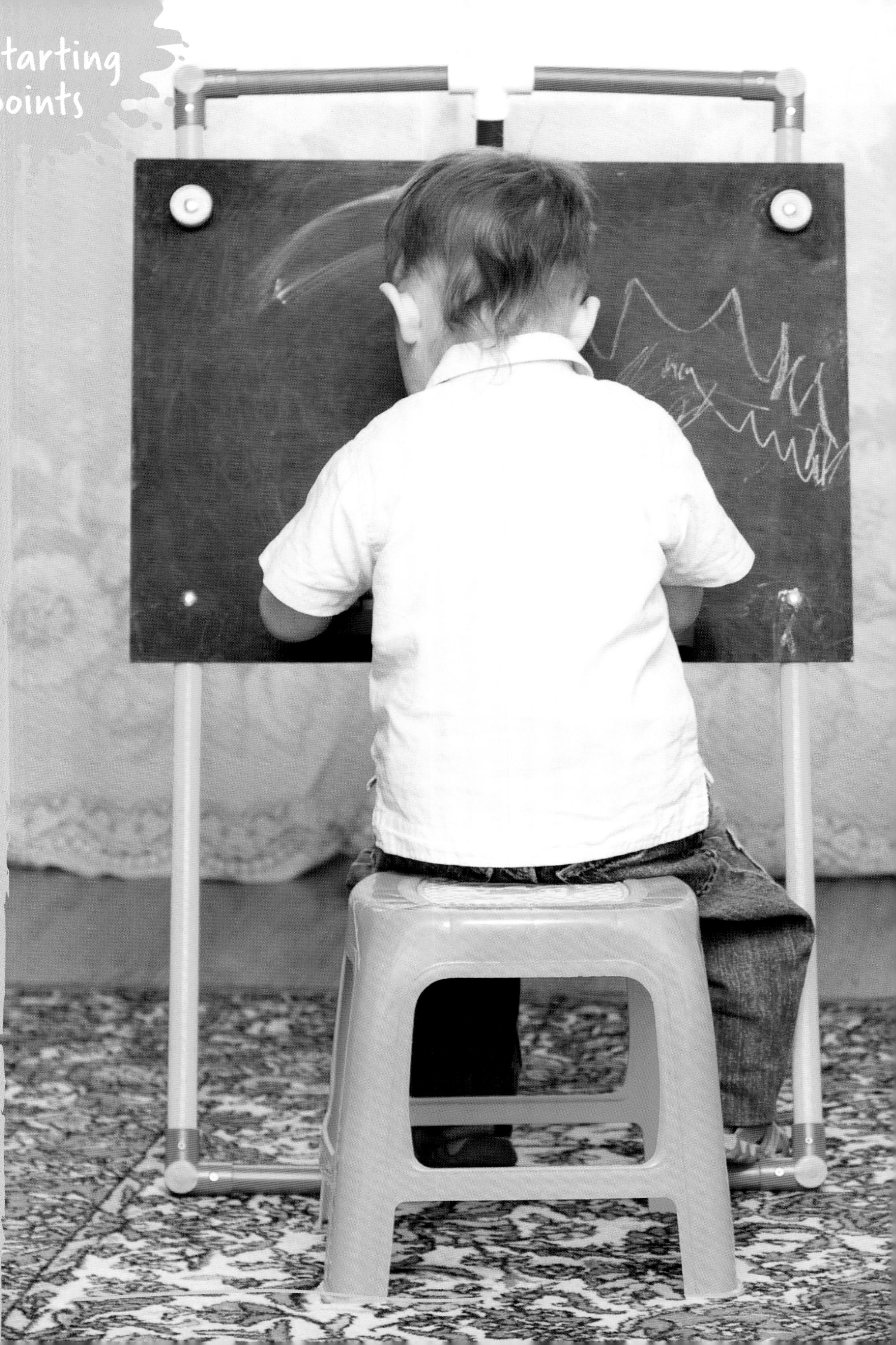

Starting points

Before we begin to explore the range of skills, knowledge, motivations and attitudes that go together in order for a child to learn to write, it's important to think about what an effective approach to education in the early years looks like. This is a very particular and special time in a child's development – it is a non-statutory phase, before a child's compulsory education begins. It is a time to explore, to wonder, to play, to laugh, and to experience the joy of learning. We need to consider where we stand on child-initiated versus adult-directed learning for the different ages within the phase, and also think about the crucial role of play. We need to think about how we can resource our settings, to make the most of every opportunity for learning. We need to explore how we can create an effective 'enabling environment' in which the resources act as an additional teacher. We need to remember that the early years is about the care, learning and development of each unique child – it is not simply some kind of preparation for later schooling. The children's personal, social, emotional and physical development is as important as their academic learning.

Early years pedagogy: who leads the learning?

As early years educators, a key aspect of our pedagogy is that it is child-centered – that it is based around the needs, interests, care and development of each individual child. It is not centered on curriculum, or testing, or results. It is about ensuring the well-being and happiness of the children who have been entrusted to our care. However, if we stop to consider, even in the most child-centered environment possible, adults are still making many of the decisions. We are typically the ones who decide what resources are on offer to the children, and where those resources are organised within the space. Even if the children are given free choice of what to play with, when and where, the choice is only really between those resources and spaces that we have within our settings. We also need to think about how and when it is appropriate to intervene with the play and learning that's happening and when to introduce a next step for each individual child.

When we are thinking about how far children should control and initiate their own learning, and how much input and direction the teacher or practitioner should give, one of the most important questions is: how will they learn this best? Clearly, there are certain skills and pieces of knowledge that are best or most easily learned by direct teaching from an adult. Equally, there are particular disciplines and skills (letter formation and handwriting being prime examples) where adult-directed practice is the most efficient way to learn. However, in the early years we need to balance the desire to 'get them learning' what we want them to learn, with an understanding of the wider development of the child, their interests, motivations and needs. We must also remember that this is a non statutory phase, and that our children have the right to play, to make their own choices, and to take ownership of their learning.

Finding a balance

0–2 years

For babies and toddlers, the focus is on care, attachment with a key person, and all the wonderful learning that comes out of a small child exploring their world. The adults will offer resources which the baby or toddler can respond to with all their senses, taking great care to avoid any choke hazards. Babies are just starting to make sense of the world around them, building their core strength, and learning to explore. High quality talk is vital at this age, as at all other times in the early years, to help children start to understand what the people around them are saying.

2–3 years

For these young children, it's appropriate and sensible to stick mainly to child-initiated learning – to respond, react to and build on the child's interests. The adult might initiate some activities that would benefit the child, or offer fresh experiences, but there is no insistence that these must be accessed or completed. Children of this age can show a surprising amount of extended focus when caught up in a sensory experience or a challenge. There is so much about the world that they want to discover and explore.

3–4 years

For preschool aged children, and those who will move into a Reception class in the following academic year, a mixture of mostly child-initiated, some adult-initiated and some adult-directed learning is appropriate. The higher attaining children or older children within the group will be able to focus on adult-initiated or adult-directed activities for part of the time they are with you, and you can capitalise on this to provide stretch and challenge.

4–5 years

Once the children reach the last year of the phase, and move towards the compulsory part of their education, they are typically ready to learn with more adult direction. For Reception children aged 4–5 years, adult-directed or guided learning becomes an important feature of the school day, along with time to play and initiate their own learning. There are some key skills that the children are best taught, for instance, they won't discover correct letter formation by stumbling across the skills required. They will need to practise and persevere.

5–6 years and beyond

As children move into the first Key Stage in England, they typically encounter a more formal style of learning, although some schools continue with a more child-led focus into Year 1 and beyond. Certainly, there is typically more whole class teaching with this age group, and the children should be able to focus on listening to adults for longer periods of time. They will be practising writing skills, such as handwriting, on a regular basis. They might do this as a whole class, individually or in small groups. There should still be plenty of chances for the children to have input into the direction of the learning, and to take ownership of the activities that they do.

Guiding the children's learning

Even the most child-initiated learning does not mean that the adult simply stands back and does nothing, or only joins in with the child if asked. The practitioners still have a key role to play within this type of learning because they can guide the children based on their knowledge and understanding of individuals, of how children learn and of the world. The quality of the children's experience can be greatly enhanced by:

- The way that we set up activities, areas and resources, and whether the environment inspires the children to want to explore and learn.

- How effective we are at observing the children and working out what they might need or want to learn about next.

- How well we plan experiences that allow or encourage children to learn these 'next steps'.

- How clever we are at incorporating and extending a child's interests in the activities we offer.

- The kind of resources we are able to offer, and how creatively we use these resources.

- How well we use talk to develop children's thinking and encourage them to question, explore and examine the world around them.

- How easily the children can access the resources and make decisions about what, where and how to learn.

Resources for mark making

One of the key questions to consider is how best we can use resources to create an environment that enables and encourages effective learning. This is not to say that you have to spend a fortune on buying brand new pens and paints, or fancy paper or the latest toys – often the very best resources are very simple, open-ended ones, where the children can respond with imagination, creativity and lateral thinking. Many of the best resources can be created or developed for little or no money. Because resources play such a key part in the learning that children do, it's important to think carefully about what makes a 'good' resource. The best resources tend to:

- Have a variety of uses, purposes and possibilities – they can be used in a range of different ways.

- Offer multisensory elements or features, so that they appeal to as many of the children's senses as possible.

- Be sturdy, high quality and well made, so that they will last you and your setting for a long time (this is especially important for pack-away early years settings, where they may have to be put into and out of storage each day).

- Appeal to the children, because they are interesting to touch, brightly coloured, larger than life, unusual, and so on.

- Be appropriate for the children size-wise, for instance chairs and desks that allow them to sit in the correct position to write.

The magic of multisensory resources

Given how important sensory interactions are for children's development, it is interesting to consider how many of their senses children typically use in educational settings, and which senses are the most commonly used. In school, the main senses being used are sight, hearing and touch: the children look at the teacher, the board or the book, they listen to what is being said, they hold a pencil to write. Smell and taste often take a back seat, or get forgotten about completely. In the early years, children typically get to be much more hands on and to interact with resources in a much more sensory way. As you will see throughout this book, you can offer lots of multisensory experiences to your children to enhance their mark making. For instance you might:

- Light a scented candle to create a relaxing atmosphere for learning.

- Play some music quietly in the background while the children write.

- Offer the children a 'feely bag', full of different textures to explore.

- Use photos, film or paintings to inspire a response, perhaps based around different writing genres.

- Blindfold volunteers, to smell or taste some foods.

- Write 'letters in the air' using torches (or light sabers!) in a darkened room or a blacked out tent.

Plastic versus natural resources

Plastic toys and resources tend to dominate many children's homes and are a feature of many early years settings. Generally speaking, there is quite a bit of negativity towards plastic toys within the sector, and in recent years in society more generally, as people become ever more aware of their environmental cost. Plastic resources do however have some advantages, in that they are:

- Hygienic and easy to keep clean.

- Long lasting.

- Safe.

- Typically cheap to buy.

- Can be very life-like, for example plastic foods.

- Can help you offer a range of cultural resources, for example life-like babies from different ethnic backgrounds.

- Are often popular with the children (a set of pink plastic ponies are a big hit at our preschool and staff refuse point blank to get rid of them).

On the downside, plastic toys and resources:

- Have a limited sensory appeal for the children.

- Are not environmentally friendly to produce.

- Can use bright 'unreal' colours.

- Tend to have a limited range of uses.

- Can sometimes be stereotyped towards one gender.

However, this is not to say that plastic toys and resources do not have a valuable role to play within your setting, nor that we should be sniffy about using them. Consider the humble Lego® brick, which was voted 'Toy of the Century' just before the turn of the millennium. Lego® is a fantastic resource which can help your children develop a myriad of skills – building, construction, creativity, role play and so on and on.

Wooden toys and resources made of natural rather than man-made materials, seem to be instinctively appealing to early years educators. We want our children to connect with the natural world and to have access to a range of sensory experiences, particularly around touch and texture. Toys and resources made of natural materials have a range of advantages and benefits. Typically they:

- Offer wider sensory possibilities for the children.

- Are an environmentally-friendly alternative (so long as they are made from sustainable sources).

- Tend to use softer, pastel colours.

- Sometimes offer a wider range of uses than their plastic counterparts.

- Are often made with a specific multicultural learning purpose in mind, for instance cotton role play clothes from countries around the world.

However, on the downside, they:

- Can be harder to keep clean or to sanitise than their plastic counterparts.

- Perhaps surprisingly, are often not particularly long lasting (we've had trouble with the longevity of wooden balance bikes and wooden screens).

- Are often much more expensive to buy than their plastic counterparts.

- Can require more maintenance, for example a wooden climbing frame may need annual checks and repairs.

- Can lack some of the life-like qualities of plastic alternatives, for example wooden foods tend to look less real.

- Are not necessarily as popular with the children, who tend not to have the same warm attachment adults might have to 'real' (i.e. wooden) toys.

The ultimate guide to mark making in the early years

Using real objects

Some pedagogical approaches to early years, such as Montessori, advocate the use of real objects wherever possible. Rather than children learning to use toy versions of every day objects, the idea is that they get used to handling and using the real thing as a natural part of their learning and development. This means using real versions of plates, cups, locks, keys, foods, and so on.

There are a number of benefits to using real objects:

- The learning is real and true to life.

- There are many chances for multisensory exploration.

- Children become more confident and independent in handling and using these objects in their day-to-day lives.

- Many of these real life objects are great for developing the fine motor skills and dexterity that are needed for writing – for instance using knives for cutting, proper gardening or woodwork tools.

- Children learn to manage 'real life' risk and to understand how to handle objects with care.

- Seeing real life objects in an educational situation tends to fully engage and interest the children.

Equally, as with all types of resources, there are some downsides or potential issues to consider:

- There may be risks involved in handling real objects, for instance in using china cups or plates, where there is a risk of breakage.

- Storage can be an issue, particularly with fragile or perishable items.

- Parents and carers may feel nervous about their children using real objects.

To minimise any risks when using real objects it is wise to:

- Use them in small groups or one-to-one with individuals.

- Ensure that there is close adult supervision and that adults are trained in their usage, for instance with wood working tools.

- Consider opting for 'child size' versions of adult tools (for instance at preschool we use 'Gardener's Apprentice' tools on the allotment — these are high quality versions of adult tools made in a child's size).

- Take an overview of any other activities that are going on while you have real objects on offer — aim to pre-empt any potential issues, for instance a particularly lively activity next to your priceless tea set.

- Reassure any worried parents about your risk assessment policies and procedures and how closely staff will supervise the children.

- Think about any children in your setting who have Special Educational Needs and Disabilities (SEND) — is it appropriate and safe for them to use these real objects? If not, will they feel excluded from an activity and how could you overcome this?

The ultimate guide to mark making in the early years

Repurposed and handmade resources

As well as real objects, make the most of any repurposed materials and resources that you can get hold of – recycled, organic or natural materials that you have to hand, objects that you find outside, or resources that you make yourself. Repurposed materials are typically great for their multi-purpose nature – you can use them to build dens, screen off a reading area, make a space rocket, create seats or inspire art – the only limit really is your and your children's imaginations! These materials are often either free to get hold of, or very cheap.

They include:

- Large pieces of material – choose a whole range of types for maximum adaptability, including see through materials, such as net and gauze (try charity shops for cheap net curtains), camouflage style materials, including nets, large bed sheets or tarpaulins for den building and materials from a range of cultures, for instance sari fabric or material with an African print.

- Cardboard boxes – ask parents to bring in any spares, or visit a packaging or storage company for those giant wardrobe-sized boxes.

- Large flat sheets of cardboard (for instance those used for packaging A1 flipcharts).

- Spare building or garden landscaping materials: rocks, bricks, pebbles, sections of drainpipe, reels.

- Natural 'found' materials, ones that you have grown yourself or sourced from others (e.g. approach a local tree surgeon for some logs), including pine cones, pumpkin seeds, leaves, conkers, sticks, tree trunks and sections of log (great for seats and stepping stones).

Take your children for a walk to gather found materials, or ask parents to collect these with their children, to bring in. Ask local businesses (DIY stores, builders' merchants, offices) whether you can take any spare materials off their hands. There is an organisation called 'Scrapstore' that offers a huge range of cheap recycled materials for early years settings, schools and charities. See the companion website for details.

When you're considering a new resource for your setting or classroom, don't always turn to the latest catalogue of resources. It's my experience that the children love resources that you make for them yourself. It says something special when you put your own time and effort into making a resource for the class. In the past, I've made a 'noise-o-meter' and a 'weather rewards chart' among others.

Displaying real resources

Small children find a special kind of fascination in the objects, items and creatures that they discover, especially the ones they find outside. A strange shaped stone becomes a 'dinosaur's tooth'; a piece of muddy quartz is washed and becomes a priceless 'crystal'; a flattened hedgehog is studied as you pass it on the road each day. A lovely idea is to make or buy a 'Cabinet of Curiosities' – a cabinet where the children can display their found objects and which could inspire many different kinds of writing.

ORGANISING AND ACCESSING RESOURCES

Resources are most useful, and most likely to be used, when staff and children can access them easily. The way that you organise your resources will depend a great deal on the kind of setting you're in, the storage spaces you have available and the age group with which you work. Whatever your situation, there are certain key features of a well organised set of resources:

- Keep them tidy and clean, by having a regular time when you sort through, wash and reorganise them.

- Label the boxes or trays when you store them, using both visual symbols and written labels.

- If a resource has not been used for 6–12 months or more, either use it the following day or give it away.

- Never keep things 'just in case' they might come in handy at some undefined point in the future.

- Edit your resources regularly – often they build up over time as you add more new items.

- Be ruthless with yourself – once a year, get all your resources out and work your way through them. Prioritise what you keep according to how useful it is for learning, and also how often it is used, rather than how much you love it. Stop when your cupboards are full then steel yourself to get rid of all the rest.

- Less is more when it comes to resources – that way things get used in a more creative way, and are likely to be treated more carefully. Aim for uncluttered methods of storage and organisation, rather than ramming every last item into your cupboards.

- Find ways to make the resources as accessible as possible to your children, so that they can make genuine choices about what they'd like to play with. (See the sections opposite for advice on making this happen.)

- Keep an up-to-date inventory – often there will be fantastic resources that you didn't know were there, had forgotten about or that you simply could not find.

Day-to-day storage

Many early years settings and primary schools give each child a way to store his or her day-to-day items. A storage unit with a set of named plastic trays, one per child, is usually the best solution. Book bags, learning journeys, paintings, WOW slips, newsletters and so on can all be stored in the child's tray, to take home at the end of each day. The child's name should be clearly labelled on the front of the tray, preferably with a photo alongside that is familiar to the child. The same photo can be used on the child's peg, and on a registration board as well. Children, parents and staff can use these trays to exchange notes with each other.

Resources and pack-away settings

If you're in a pack-away early years setting, where you have to put all your resources away at the end of each session, you need to think creatively about how you store and access resources. You will have to be ruthless about the quantity and type of those resources you put into storage each day. In a pack-away setting it can be hard to offer the children free choice of resources because the adults need to resource the environment before the children arrive. However, there are still a number of ways in which you can increase choice and ownership for the children:

- Have a 'choices' book or board, with a selection of laminated photos that show the resources available, so that the children can choose from these.

- Have clear boxes in your cupboards, clearly labelled with a photo on the front, and take children in to choose their own resources.

- Use 'wheel out' units with clear trays in them, again labelled with photos of what's inside.

When you're setting up your continuous provision for the day, a good idea is to leave a space labelled 'Children's Choice'. Consult with the children first thing in the morning to find out what they would like set out in that space each day.

The space as a resource

The space you have, and the way that you lay it out, has a powerful impact on the children's experiences within that space. A key factor in learning to write is feeling inspired to make marks in the first place but also being able to focus and concentrate effectively. Your children will learn best (and you will teach them best) if your space:

- Feels bright and open, with plenty of natural daylight and easy access to the outdoors.

- Is uncluttered and easy to move around, both for practitioners and children.

- Has clearly divided areas for different types of learning or for different activities (you could use physical dividers, for example screens, but equally you can use different kinds of flooring to delineate areas).

- Has a communal space (usually a rug) where the whole group can meet to share news and listen to stories.

- Ensures comfortable levels of noise, with quiet areas as well as busy ones.

- Provides areas for reflection, for instance a comfortable sofa where children can sit to chat or read a book.

You can use the Space as a resource checklist, and the Space and communication audit at the end of the book to think more about how you use your space, and how it enhances or discourages mark making and writing (see pp. 142—143).

Displays within the space

Displays are a great way of making your space feel inviting and welcoming, and to support the development of communication and literacy skills. When children see print and symbols around the place, this helps them to learn that marks convey meaning. For instance, you might display a 'Welcome' poster in a variety of different community languages. Displays also offer a great way of celebrating your children's writing — effectively publishing their learning for all to see. Seeing their mark making on the wall of the classroom, nursery or preschool is a motivating factor for children of any age. Your mark making displays might include:

- Alphabet displays — the larger the better (one display per letter if possible).

- Displays of phonemes you've been working on.

- Word 'bank' displays, for instance a set of topic words or sentence openers for older writers.

- Displays to support the children's handwriting (how to form letters, how to join handwriting).

- Displays to support staff (e.g. questions to ask, cues for observations).

- Examples of the children's mark making/writing.

The ultimate guide to mark making in the early years

Top tips for displays

Get creative with the way that you present displays and where you put them. Don't use them as wallpaper – make sure that you change them regularly and that they relate to the learning that is currently going on. Displaying children's work can act as a powerful motivator – you are, in effect, 'publishing' it. Here are some top tips for how to be creative with your mark making display:

- Hang net curtain wire along the walls and peg displays onto this.

- Use room dividers for a dual purpose, adding displays to each side.

- Hang lines across your room, to peg up words, ideas or pictures.

- Use mini wooden craft pegs to peg up writing on a smaller scale (e.g. a line of string on which the children peg up a series of images from a story in the correct order).

- Display words and images in unusual places – on the ceiling, under a table, on the side of a shed.

- Graphic displays can work well in catching the eye (e.g. a pure black and white or black and silver display looks very striking).

- Windows can offer a great surface for displaying writing, particularly where you make use of the light shining through your displays (e.g. 'stained glass' cellophane artwork).

Key questions about displays

Displaying the children's work takes time and effort, so it's worth thinking about how you do it and, indeed, why. It's tempting to put children's work up on the walls, just to 'get it done'. It's equally tempting to put up posters or images that tick equality, diversity or British Values boxes, rather than thinking carefully about the impact on learning. Reflect on whether your displays enhance the mark making and writing activities that are done in your setting, or whether they might distract or even detract from it.

Use the following steps to ensure that your displays really make an impact on learning:

- Choose a time when there are no children in the setting.

- Step outside the room, pause and breathe deeply.

- Take a few moments to empty your mind of any preconceptions.

- Walk into the space, looking at it completely afresh.

- Aim to see it as though you are a child, viewing it for the first time.

- What do you notice? Is anything missing?

- Where is your focus drawn and why?

- Do you feel overwhelmed – is there too much going on?

- You might like to use the Displays audit (see p. 143) to examine and reflect on your displays.

The 'working wall'

A working wall is a display that you and your children create together. It is a work in progress rather than a finished product. You gradually add to the working wall before and during a topic or area of learning, referring to it as you go. It's a bit like those whiteboards that you see in a detective drama – as the evidence, facts and suspects in the case are discovered, the whiteboard gets covered with writing. The working wall can help children understand how to make connections between ideas within their writing, because it acts as a kind of giant mind map of their thinking. Your working wall might be:

- Based on a 'letter of the week' – the children could add words starting with this letter, bring in pictures of objects that begin with it and record themselves saying the letter sound on 'talking buttons'.

- Created around a mind map on a class topic, e.g. The Great Fire of London – as you study the topic, the children could add in images of key characters, key vocabulary and a map of London at the time.

- Based on a story, e.g. *The Gruffalo* (Julia Donaldson and Axel Scheffler, Macmillan, 1999) – the children could build up an image of the key characters (e.g. adding tusks and warts to the Gruffalo), pin up the sequence of events in the story and write out key phrases.

- Designed to gather facts or information over the course of studying a topic. For instance, when looking at growth in science, you could start with a large picture of a plant, then label this, add colour and facts about how plants grow, and so on.

Staff as a resource

Within an early years setting such as a preschool or a nursery, there may be a fairly large number of staff working alongside each other or in a series of different rooms. In a mainstream school environment, the setting is more likely to be a classroom space and, because the ratio requirements are less, there is likely to be fewer adults (a teacher and perhaps one or two support staff). The staff you have are the very best resource in supporting children's mark making. To get the best out of your staff:

- Encourage your staff to see themselves as a team – talk about 'us' and 'we' rather than 'I' and 'you'.

- Plan together, as a team, focusing on the best interests of the children.

- Look for the best in others, supporting and encouraging those who need development, and trying not to slip into criticism or negativity.

- See continued training and development as a key aim for your team.

- Capitalise on the interests of staff, as well as of children – for instance, if someone is particularly interested in Makaton, encourage them to pursue that interest by organising training.

- Share your skills and knowledge around – where a member of staff is particularly skilled in an area, get them to disseminate that information to your team.

- Delegate responsibility, to encourage staff to feel a sense of ownership.

Getting parents involved

The more closely you can involve parents in their children's learning, the better the chances are that your children's writing will develop well. Ironically, it's often the case in education that it's easy enough to reach those parents who do the 'right things' for their children at home, but it's much harder to reach those parents who most need your help and support. In my experience, one of the keys to working with parents is to make them feel welcome, and to keep doing it, over and over again. Throw down the invitations to get involved one after another but try not to feel disappointed if they don't take you up on your offers. Take great care not to come across as patronising, nor to appear to tell others how they should bring up their children or what they are getting wrong. Instead, take the same approaches that work with young children: persistence, belief, praise, positivity, creativity and then more persistence.

To get parents involved:

- Invite them in regularly to see presentations by staff and children, to attend fundraising events, and to take part in workshops.

- Use lots of different ways to communicate, and do it frequently and informally.

- Send home newsletters, and make sure these offer information and advice, rather than just requests to label clothing or lists of complaints.

- Set up a website and preferably a blog as well, so that parents can find out what the children are doing day-to-day in the setting.

- Use texts, emails and social media messages as a form of instant communication.

So now that we've had a chance to think about pedagogy and resources, it's time to set off with the children on the magical journey that leads to becoming a writer.

Part 1

I know how to communicate

In this section

- Consider verbal and non-verbal communication

- 'Read' what your children say – even whey they are not talking

- Enhance the role of talk in your setting

- Encourage your children to listen better

- Understand how to use high quality talk

Consider this...

The urge to communicate our needs, thoughts, ideas, wishes or opinions is there from the moment we are born. We hear it in the cries of a tired, hungry or teething baby, or the tantrums of a toddler. Even before we can form words, we still let people know what we feel, through gestures, expressions and noises. Right from the start, babies are building a network of connections between their brain cells (neurons). The more that people talk with and stimulate them, the more of these connections are formed. Children who experience a rich environment, full of varied sensory experiences and lots of high quality talk, will become better and more confident communicators.

Early language development is crucial for both speaking and writing – all the time we are talking we are picking up the vocabulary, grammar and patterns of meaning that make up our language. When we begin to make marks to communicate, it is the things that we say and think that we are trying to express. The better our verbal communication, the more fluently we will be able to express ourselves in writing. Even if a child does not have access to a rich, varied and talk-filled environment before they arrive at your setting, your input still has the potential to make a huge difference.

Face, hands, body – non-verbal communication

Imagine for a moment that you are a baby again. Your world is a strange, confusing place full of big creatures that make noises you don't understand. There are some familiar faces – mummy, daddy, big brother, grandma – and you quickly learn and respond to these faces. You begin to understand that a smile means you make someone happy, and you can pick out the sound and smell of mum and dad. When you feel hungry, you need to get these big creatures to understand. So, you use sound (waaahhh!), combined with an instinctive gesture (a sucking movement of your lips) to get your message across.

Even before they can speak, babies make use of facial expression, gestures, signs and sounds to help us understand. A one-year-old might wave goodbye to grandma, or point at a toy that she can't reach. Even before they understand individual words, children are 'reading' what we say, through how we look as well as how we sound. One of the key skills of the early years educator is the ability to communicate in both verbal and non-verbal ways. All the time you show your children that spoken language (and its close friend, non-verbal communication) is a great way to get a message across.

To make the most of non-verbal communication:

- Use a bright, open face and a genuine smile, to show the children that you like them.

- Exaggerate your use of tone – sound *very* happy, *very* interested, *very* surprised – young children are learning to read expressions so will benefit from this emphasis.

- Really *listen* to what your children tell you: be open to what they actually say rather than listening in order to talk.

- Become sensitive to non-verbal clues that tell you about a child's emotions or needs.

- Adapt your approach as you read these clues and cues.

The ultimate guide to mark making in the early years

A key skill for the early years practitioner is learning how to join in with a game or activity, without putting the children off or causing them to 'freeze up'. To get it right:

Do

- Observe for a moment before moving into the play, to get a feel for what is going on. Tune into what the children are saying to each other.

- Use a question to introduce yourself into the play – 'Do you mind if I join in?' or 'Wow, that looks exciting, can I have a go?'.

- Maintain a bright, interested tone and open facial expression.

- Immediately come down to the children's level, crouching beside them rather than standing above them.

- Encourage the children to give you orders and instructions by asking questions about what is going on.

- Play around with language while you're involved with the play – for instance singing a song that relates to what they are doing, or playing around with letter sounds, e.g. 'Elijah's tower is tall and terribly tremendous!'

- Sometimes, start to play yourself, and wait for the children to join you. This is a useful technique for encouraging the children to access an area in your continuous provision that they wouldn't immediately choose for themselves. The children will almost inevitably be drawn towards what the practitioner is doing.

Don't

- Impose your own ideas, instructions or rules on the children's play, e.g. 'You should do it like this...'.

- Jump in with a closed question, designed to test for a right/wrong answer, e.g. 'How many blocks are in your tower, Elijah?'. This tends to have the effect of closing down the play.

- Step suddenly out of the play to note down an observation for the child's learning journey/profile. Respect the play enough to only leave it when it's finished.

How talk develops

Babies cry to communicate what they want. At first it is hard for new parents to tell what their baby wants – is it food, sleep, attention, a fresh nappy? As the baby and parents get to know each other, it becomes easier for them to distinguish one cry from another, with non-verbal cues providing helpful information too. The first year of a child's life can feel like a guessing game in which you try to anticipate what your crying baby needs. Learning to talk involves developing the physical muscles in and around the mouth that allow us to make sounds. Language is learned rather than genetic – babies are born with the ability to *speak any language*. The language they speak (and the accent they use) depends on the words they hear in those early weeks, months and years. Sounds and words are formed with the tongue, teeth, lips, palate and vocal chords.

Speaking is intrinsically linked to hearing. Babies and young children hear others speaking to and around them, and then emulate these sound patterns. This is why it is so important that young children are given a hearing test – hearing problems can very quickly become language development problems. As a practitioner working with young children, you should be on the look out for any signs that there could be problems with a child's hearing. Glue ear is a particularly common problem in this age group. Be alert to the issues described below, as these can point to a problem with hearing:

- A child doesn't respond when you call their name, especially if their back is turned to you.

- A child appears to daydream and often doesn't seem to have listened properly to instructions.

- A child talks more loudly than you might expect.

- A child mispronounces a number of different words.

- A child seems grumpy, upset or frustrated much of the time.

Developing complex speech patterns

Spoken language is full of rules, although we're not really aware that we're following these when we speak in our first language. As children learn to speak, they quickly add grammatical constructs to what they are saying. Those first few words: 'dadda', 'mamma', 'ball' are nouns, but the child soon adds verbs to the mix: 'mamma get ball' and then pronouns: 'mummy get me the ball'. Amazingly, from about three years onwards, children can adapt the way that they speak so that it's appropriate to a situation, for instance using different speech patterns with a friend than they do with a grown up.

It's important to be aware of the normal patterns of speech development so that you can spot any signs that a child might be having problems. Bear in mind, though, that some children remain non-verbal for longer than others, with some appearing to be lagging in their speech development, but then jumping a stage. You can download a copy of the table opposite from the companion website. (website)

Typical development of speech

Young babies (pre-linguistic stage)

- Makes eye contact with those who are speaking
- Uses facial expressions to interact with others
- Uses noises to communicate emotions

12 months plus

- Uses one or more words
- Points to something and names it

18 months plus

- Learns up to 10 new words a day
- Puts two or three word sentences together
- Starts to use some grammatical constructions

2 years plus

- Learns new words very quickly
- Starts to include pronouns: I, me, you
- Starts to string nouns and verbs together into sentences
- Begins to use plurals
- Uses questions frequently

3 years plus

- People other than parents can understand speech
- Begins to hold sustained conversations
- Adapts tone, speech patterns and words depending on who she is talking with
- Says name and his age
- Talks to self while playing

4 years plus

- Can narrate a sequence of events ('First we ..., then we ...')
- Uses language with his peers to share, take turns, squabble
- Starts to use language to describe other people's emotions (empathy)
- Ask lots of questions
- Speech clearly understandable, with few mistakes

5 years plus

- Creates properly constructed sentences when speaking
- Has a wide vocabulary
- Can offer opinions during a discussion

Learning how to listen

Learning how to communicate is as much about learning how to listen as it is about learning how to talk. Children develop their speech through imitating what other people say, and so it is vital that they learn to tune into it and listen effectively. This phonological awareness is also very important in learning to read, because it will allow them to match units of sound (phonemes) to units of writing (graphemes). Make sure that listening is a skill you talk about and practise regularly. Introduce displays about listening and create opportunities for children to practise their listening in lots of different contexts, throughout the day. You might:

* Use a soundtrack on a listening centre to identify different animal noises.

* Listen to a recording of different bird songs; go outside to see if you can identify any specific birds.

* Have a variety of telephones, both old and new (children especially love the 'old style' handsets with a dial/receiver) to encourage role playing conversations in shops, offices, etc.

* Go on a 'listening walk' around your local area – you could record the sounds that you hear.

* Get a group to practise being completely silent, using a 'Statues' or 'Sleeping Lions' game.

* Use 'talk partners' to give children the chance to share their ideas and thinking with each other.

* Have 'chat buddies' or 'conversation buddies' – times when you encourage the children to engage in sustained social chatting with their friends, for instance at snack time or just before break.

activity

TALK ABOUT LISTENING

YOU WILL NEED

* A carpet or circle time session

LEARNING INTENTIONS

* To encourage the children to think about what 'good listening' means

* To improve focus, concentration and motivation to listen well

* To enhance learning generally, through focusing on listening behaviour

INSTRUCTIONS

Talk about 'good listening behaviour' during carpet time. Your key questions might include:

* How can we tell if someone is listening to us?

* Why is it important to sit still and keep our hands and feet to ourselves when we are on the carpet?

* What should we do if we want to ask something, or to answer a question?

* Why is it important not to talk when someone else is speaking?

The ultimate guide to mark making in the early years

Practitioner talk

You, and your colleagues, are the most valuable resource that your early years setting or primary school has to offer, and one of the most valuable things that you can give to your children is the gift of high quality talk. When you are talking to children, ensure that they can see your face so that they can watch and copy the movements that your mouth makes as you form the sounds. Use your eyes to engage and interest your children, and your tone of voice to keep them focused.

Why *what* you say matters

What you say, that is the actual words that you use, plays an important part in helping your children become adept and confident communicators. Aim to praise effort over achievement – this is the best way to motivate children to try harder and to achieve their best. Be specific about what you say, particularly when you praise a child for doing something well. For instance, instead of saying:

'That's a really great painting, Tariq, you're such a good artist. Aren't you a clever boy!'

Try saying:

'Wow, I can see that you've worked really hard on your painting Tariq. You really stuck at it. I love the way you've used red to show the volcano spurting out lava.'

When it comes to using talk, one common habit we can fall into is to constantly refer to the gender of the child saying 'good girl'/'good boy'. We might not even be aware that we are doing this. We can also find ourselves using specific vocabulary depending on whether we are talking to or about a boy/girl (strong for a boy versus feisty for a girl). It's easy to fall into these linguistic habits, and they can be hard to overcome. Aim to 'hear yourself' as you speak, to catch yourself using gendered language.

Most of the time, it's best to model 'proper' talk for the children rather than mirroring the patterns of early speech. 'Baby talk' has its use for comforting young children when they are upset, but most of the time we should model language being used accurately. That's not to say we should be using complex, adult level terminology, but we do need to use the correct grammatical constructions and vocabulary that will stretch and challenge our children.

Self-talk and parallel-talk

All the time, you are introducing new vocabulary into your children's worlds. Demonstrate to the children how you can say the same thing in lots of different ways and with different kinds of vocabulary. A great way to do this is to use both self and parallel-talk. These techniques involve giving a running commentary of what you and your children are doing and what you are observing, as you go along. By doing this, you demonstrate patterns of speech (for example the use of time connectives). For instance, you might say:

'I can see that first you painted the balloon red. Now you are painting the sky blue. Which part are you going to paint next?'

This technique is particularly useful for children who have English as an Additional Language (EAL), as it introduces them to common patterns of speech and to new vocabulary. You can use self and parallel-talk to introduce a huge variety of words. For instance, when talking about a tower that a child is building, you might incorporate words such as:

'tall, taller, tallest, high, higher, highest, tower, towering, skyscraper, build, built, building, construct, construction, structure, strong, weak'.

Develop the vocabulary of mark making with your children, using words such as:

'line, draw, write, scribble, doodle, note, jot down, mark, record, note down, list, register'.

Why *how* you speak matters

It's not just the content of your speech that is important for your children, it is also your tone of voice (how you say what you say). Remember, not all of your children will understand all the vocabulary you use all the time, and they will therefore have to rely on tone to figure out meaning. This is especially so if you teach children who have EAL, or if you work with very young children or babies. We can tune into a person's emotional state through the sound of their voice (or prosody) and we can also gather social information. We can tell whether someone is unhappy, or disinterested, or kind, or excited or surprised, simply through picking up on aural clues and cues.

Interestingly, vocal tone stimulates the parts of the brain that are connected to our emotional state. In other words, if I sound happy, you are likely to feel happy too. Remember, you don't have to actually *be* happy or excited to *sound* happy or excited. As a practitioner or teacher this is one of the key skills that you can use to enhance your communication – adding warmth, variety and interest to the way that you sound.

activity

COMMUNICATING THROUGH TONE

YOU WILL NEED

- A staff training day
- Several members of staff

LEARNING INTENTIONS

- To help practitioners develop their use of tone when speaking with children
- To show that *how* you say something matters a great deal

INSTRUCTIONS

Divide your staff up into pairs: one person is going to role play the child while the other plays the adult. The scenario is that the child is playing, and the practitioner is asking questions or giving encouragement. The staff can only use consecutive numbers to communicate, no words – as few or as many numbers at a time as they wish. For instance the first person might say '1, 2, 3', the second '4', the first '5, 6', then the second '7, 8, 9, 10'.

The idea is to communicate, and have a clear conversation, simply through the use of vocal tone. A person watching should be able to tell what the conversation is about despite the lack of words.

The ultimate guide to mark making in the early years

Developing talk in your setting

Imaginative talk

Young children love to use their imaginations, and will respond well to talk that is supposedly coming from a toy or a puppet. Create pretend conversations between you and the puppet, or the toy and the child, as this will support imaginative development that is crucial for storytelling. Children may also talk more freely to a puppet than they might do to an adult.

Mistakes in speech

Young children will quite often say words incorrectly, or have trouble making particular sounds. Where a child makes mistakes in speech, for instance saying a word incorrectly, model the correct word, rather than highlighting the mistake. So, if a child says:

'I builded it.'

You could say...

'Yes, you built it, well done!'

Similarly, if a child mispronounces a word ('lellow' instead of 'yellow' is a common mispronunciation), repeat the word back properly, but again do not highlight that a mistake was made. Some mispronunciations can simply be about the child developing the mouth and face muscles required to say the sound. However, if a child makes repeated errors, or continues to mispronounce a letter or letter combination over a longer period of time, refer them for a speech and language assessment. There may be a physical problem with speech or hearing that needs to be addressed by a specialist intervention.

Language delay

Most children don't just 'grow out of' language problems. It's vital for your children that you identify any issues early on, and arrange intervention to help them develop their skills. A month of intervention in the early years can be the equivalent to six months input later on. If you find it hard to understand what a child is saying, particularly by the age of 3, then it is likely that there is some kind of issue with language development. The younger the child, the more impact intervention has so flag up any concerns you have sooner rather than later.

Remember, too, that a child with language delay will be impacted in other areas of learning and development. The child may find it harder to socialise and make friends because they cannot join in easily with games or conversations. The child is likely to find it hard to learn at the same rate as their peers, and will almost certainly read and write later than is normal. Sometimes, a language delay can indicate that the child has a special need (such as being on the autistic spectrum, or having attention deficit disorder) that will impact on other areas of development as well.

There are various reasons why a child's language development might be delayed – sometimes related to hearing, but not always. Remember that hearing issues can develop after a hearing test has been given, and that testing and diagnosis can be patchy depending on where you are in the country. In some areas, young children have their hearing and language development checked several times. In other local authorities this does not happen at all.

Language delay may be caused by:

- An undiagnosed hearing impairment.

- Delayed oral motor development (i.e. the muscles needed for speech have not developed properly).

- Issues with the brain or central nervous system.

- Issues with physical, psychological or cognitive development.

- Social and emotional issues, for instance anxiety can be a factor in selective mutism.

- Specific special needs, such as an autistic spectrum condition or a sensory processing disorder.

It is vital to highlight any concerns you have, and to explain to parents why it's so important to identify and treat language delay early on. Parents can react negatively to being told that their child has what they perceive to be 'a problem'. Share information about language development, and explain how positive the outcomes can be for the child where an early intervention happens.

HOSTING A PARENT/CARER WORKSHOP

activity

YOU WILL NEED

- Several teachers/practitioners to present/run activities
- An audience of interested parents
- A computer/laptop, data projector and screen
- Resources for several different language activities you currently do at your setting

LEARNING INTENTIONS

- To help parents understand more about how language develops
- To encourage parents to understand what language delay is
- To encourage parents to support communication, language and literacy at home

INSTRUCTIONS

Host a parent/carer workshop on communication, language and literacy. At pre-school, we did this in response to questions from parents about early language development, and queries about why we were not getting the children to sit and trace over their names (our parents felt this constituted 'writing properly'). We realised that parents needed more information about how young children learn to write. We also had concerns about the number of children who were coming into our setting with weak language skills.

In the workshop we used PowerPoint slides, as well as some quick challenges for parents (how many words a child would know at different ages), and some activities for them to do with their children, for instance fine motor activities such as threading and weaving.

Find useful resources to support your parent workshop on the companion website: the PowerPoint presentation we used at our preschool for the parent workshop and a leaflet we created for parents to take away with them. (website)

Part 2

I can physically make marks

In this section

- Help your children build muscle strength – both fine and gross motor skills

- Encourage your children to develop their dexterity

- Improve your children's eye to hand coordination

- Help your children develop a tripod pencil grip

Consider this...

We develop the ability to control our bodies from the head downwards and from the centre of the body outwards. In other words, babies gradually strengthen their neck muscles, until they can hold their heads upright. After developing the muscles needed to roll over and sit up, they build their strength until they can crawl and then finally walk. Once children are walking, they must build strength in the entire body so that they can balance themselves to sit and write.

In the same way, a child learns to control shoulder and whole arm movements before developing close control of hands and fingers. As fine motor control develops, the child will eventually learn how to grip a writing tool and make the fine movements needed to hold a pencil and write.

Writing takes a surprising amount of hand and finger strength – think about how your hands ache when you have to write for long periods, for instance in an exam. It's important that the child has sufficient body strength to maintain a good posture when sitting to write. At this stage in their development, children need to build their whole body, hand and finger strength through a variety of different activities, not just through the act of writing itself. As well as building strength and control of their muscle movements, children must also learn to coordinate – to create the eye to hand neural connections required for writing.

Often the activities used to achieve these gross and fine motor skills appear to have nothing to do with mark making or writing as an observer might conceive of it. However, they all contribute to children being able to write, and write neatly, in the future. Share information with parents about how and why these activities are so important for young children, so that they understand the approaches you use in your setting, and also what they can do to support their child at home. Ask parents not to push their children to 'hold a pencil and write properly' before they are ready. This can do more damage than good, particularly if the child does not have the strength or coordination required.

Building whole body strength

For good posture and writing, it's vital for children to be able to support their trunk in an upright position, and keep their head supported. This requires a good sense of balance, strength in the stomach/torso muscles and in the neck and shoulders. An incorrect writing posture, or a posture in which the child supports himself by leaning on the desk, can lead to problems later on in the child's education. Physical activities help develop muscle tone, build skills such as coordination and concentration, and are important for healthy development generally. Aim to get your children using cross body movements, which support the development of right brain/left brain connections.

Gross motor activities might include:

- Balance beams
- Balance on one leg for a set time
- Obstacle courses with cones
- Crawling through tunnels
- Building and hiding in dens
- Target practice
- Climbing frames and slides
- Ride on toys
- Balance bikes
- Running races
- Skipping
- Spinning hoops

- Throwing and catching activities
- Hop scotch
- Different ways of walking – on tiptoes, forwards, backwards, sideways
- Digging in a garden area
- Carrying buckets of water/sand
- Dance sessions
- Yoga sessions
- Wheelbarrow walking
- Tug of war (with supervision)
- Trips to a local park or play area
- Monkey bars (these are wonderful for grip strength too).

Another useful tip is to get the children to write laying down on their tummies on the floor, which will support the development of upper body strength, and to get them to write laying on their backs, which will develop strength in the shoulder and upper arm muscles.

Hand press starter activity

This exercise is great for hand, arm and upper body strength. It works well as a starter activity before doing some writing:

- Get the children to stand in a space.

- Ask them to put their hands out in front of them, palms together (in a similar position to someone praying).

- Now get the children to push their palms together hard. They should feel the muscles in their arms, shoulders and upper body working.

- Hold for 5 seconds and then release.

- Repeat several times, gradually building up the amount of repetitions.

Bilateral integration – crossing the mid line

Most people have one dominamt side of their body. For the majority of us, this is the right hand (and also the right foot, right eye and so on) but for some people it's the left hand side so the reverse will be the case. When we pick up a pen that is to our left, we reach for it with our right hand, across the centre or mid line of our bodies. However, even though one side is dominant, we are able to get the two sides of our bodies to work together efficiently. This allows us to do activities such as tying a knot, where the two sides of the body are making different movements. Similarly, when kicking a ball with the dominant leg, the other leg helps balance and support the body.

Writing requires the ability to coordinate the two sides of our body – the left hand holds the paper while the right hand holds the writing tool. Similarly, we must be able to cross the midline, keeping the pen in our right hand as we move across the page, rather than swapping it from left to right at the midpoint. The reverse is true with left-handed children (see p. 50). Those children who struggle with bilateral integration may also struggle more generally with reading and writing. Incorporate activities that will help your children develop this skill.

- Play 'Simon Says'. Give instructions that require the children to cross the midline (e.g. touch your left shoulder with your right hand).

- Get the children to tap their heads, and rub their stomachs in a circular motion, at the same time.

- Ask the children to put their right hand on the left side of their nose, and their left hand on their right cheek, and then swap the two over.

- Set up an obstacle course with lots of tunnels, for the children to crawl through.

- Offer a stepladder for your children to climb, and show them how to do it using cross lateral movements.

- Encourage the children to kick a football with their non-dominant foot.

Difficulties with motor skills

There are a number of reasons why a child might struggle with motor skills. Perhaps they live in an area where there are few opportunities for outdoor play and so have not had a chance to build these skills. Perhaps it is unsafe to play outside because of a main road nearby or because the child spends a lot of time on screens. It might also be that the child has specific motor difficulties or a sensory processing disorder.

Dyspraxia

This is a term for a child who has special needs involving motor skills – the child finds it hard to organise their movements. Typically, a child with dyspraxia will appear clumsy, slow and easily distracted. The child will need help to develop the movement skills that other children grasp instinctively. Parents of a child who has dyspraxia might have noticed that their child was slow to reach the normal developmental milestones, particularly those to do with movement. Of course, writing is a skill that requires high levels of control of movement, so a child who has dyspraxia will struggle to pick it up.

As with all special needs, early identification is the key. Keep an eye out for the following problems which may indicate that a child in your setting has dyspraxia and will need additional support to access certain aspects of education:

- Finds it particularly hard to stay still.

- Tends to speak more loudly than is needed.

- Bumps into things, falls over frequently.

- Tends not to participate in imaginative and creative play.

- Finds it hard to judge levels of risk of physical activities (e.g. jumps from height).

- Flaps hands when running.

- Is a messy eater.

- Is isolated from peers.

- Has poor language development.

- Finds it hard to concentrate.

Children who have dyspraxia will find it hard to deal with an open plan area, and with high levels of visual stimulation (for instance displays hanging down from the ceiling). They will also struggle with independent skills such as getting dressed. It can be helpful for parents to give the child shoes/clothes that are easy to put on, e.g. self fastener straps on shoes rather than laces.

Supporting children with dyspraxia

There are plenty of strategies you can put in place to help a child in your setting who has dyspraxia. Look first at the environment itself – avoid strip lights and over-busy walls. Minimise sensory distractions to help the child feel more settled and relaxed. Choose activities that aid the development of motor skills, but support the child one-to-one, ensuring that you break down the skills into manageable chunks. You might:

- Offer plenty of chances to practise balance and aim – wobble boards, walking on a straight line, throwing at or into a target area.

- Give the child a visual timetable, to explain what the setting routines are and how the day is structured.

- Use visual prompts to help the child understand what the activities are, and what is coming next.

- Have a 'time out' option that the child can use if feeling stressed or in need of a break.

Building hand and finger strength

Our fingers and hands play a vital role in our daily lives, helping us perform many tasks and actions: grasping, pointing, writing, drawing, stroking, picking up, climbing and so on. About a quarter of the motor cortex (the part of the brain which controls all body movement) is dedicated to hand movement. Interestingly, we use many of the muscles in the lower arm to control our finger movements, as well as the smaller muscles within our hands.

Children naturally develop hand and finger strength during the course of their daily routine (brushing teeth, pulling on clothes). Encourage your children to be as independent as possible, for instance encouraging them to do up their coats by themselves (doing up buttons is a great for fine motor development). You can also help your children develop their strength through specific exercises and activities. Aim to develop your children's:

- Grip strength – their whole hand strength when grasping, grabbing or gripping.

- Pinch strength – the strength of the thumb and forefinger (and sometimes the middle finger too).

Those children who find it difficult to control their hands and fingers may not be able to gather the subtle sensory information that is needed to make marks with a pencil. Sometimes these children over compensate for the lack of control and feeling in their fingers, and end up grasping mark making tools too tightly. On the next page are a variety of activities that will help all your children build their hand and finger strength.

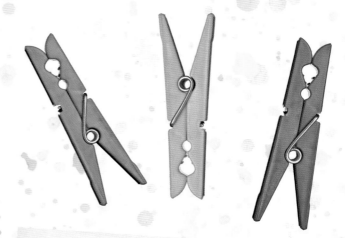

Activities for snack or lunch time

- Get the children involved in preparing foods: grating, chopping or cutting up food for snack time, or in a cookery session.

- Encourage them to squeeze oranges to make juice to have at snack time.

- Have jugs on the tables, so that children can pour their own drinks (and a cloth for mopping up any messes – squeezing out cloths is great for hand strength too).

- They could wipe their mats and tables after eating.

- Put items in your water tray that the children can squeeze: squashy toys, foam sponges, etc.

Drawing and writing activities

- Let your children draw on a vertical surface – an easel, or some paper attached to the wall. This is better for developing hand and wrist strength than drawing on a horizontal surface.

- See if they can trace a line to find the right way through a maze – both small-scale and on large sheets of paper.

- Ask for help sharpening the pencils.

- Get the children to hang up paintings to dry, or hang out 'the washing', with pegs.

Activities with sand and water

- Get the children to pour liquids from a large jug into a small one, or from a jug into a cup.

- Use a jug with measuring lines on it, and get the children to pour up to a specific line.

- Encourage them to carry buckets filled with soil, water or sand.

- See if they can squeeze wet sand together to make 'sand balls' (and fresh snow in the water tray to make snow balls if you get the chance).

- They can wash up toy plates in washing up water, with a cloth, in a role play kitchen, a water tray or in the sink.

Squashing and squishing activities

- Offer the children malleable materials to knead, squeeze and play with: play dough, clay, pastry, gloop, sand, mud.

- Encourage them to roll small pieces of clay or play dough up into tiny balls (perhaps to make 'peas' for a doll's dinner).

- See if they can scrunch up balls of newspaper and throw them into a basket.

- Can they squash a soft ball? Build up repetitions gradually: first ten, then twenty and so on.

- Move them on to using a tennis ball as hand strength increases.

- Give the children bubble wrap to pop.

- See if they can crush a whole sheet of newspaper, using only one hand.

Sports games and activities

- Get the children to face a partner, put their palms together, then push against each other.

- Organise a game of tug of war with a soft cord or rope.

- Can they squash a meat baster to blow ping pong balls around an obstacle course?

- Get the children to do 'finger push-ups' – seeing how many times they can open a peg in succession.

Activities with toys/objects

- Use pop together and pull apart toys – these are particularly good for developing pinch strength.

- Fill plastic jars with interesting objects – stars, crystals, beads, small toy animals.

- Get the children to unscrew the jar, tip out the objects, return the objects to the jar, and then screw the lid up again.

- See if they can use tongs or tweezers to pick up small toys or beads and put them in a bowl. Add a competitive element by seeing how many they can do in one minute.

- See if they can carry shopping bags in a supermarket role play area.

- Get them to post coins into a piggy bank.

- Can they sort various natural objects into different pots? Stones, leaves, acorns, etc.

- Can they turn a key to lock and unlock a door?

GARAGE ROLE PLAY

YOU WILL NEED

- An outdoor area
- Several ride on cars and other vehicles
- Water squirters (the kind used for misting plants work well)
- Cloths and sponges
- Buckets or bowls of water
- Outdoor chalks
- Clipboards and pencils
- Tools (real, as appropriate, or toy ones)
- Large blocks or crates (to raise up cars for repair)
- Tills, telephones, office equipment

LEARNING INTENTIONS

- To build the children's hand and finger strength and dexterity
- To encourage the children to practise eye to hand coordination
- To inspire mark making in a 'real life' role play scenario

INSTRUCTIONS

Set up part of your outdoor area or playground as a 'garage'. You could set this up ahead of time, or get your children to decide how they would like to lay out the areas. Mark making activities at the garage could include:

- Marking out bays for the cars with outdoor chalks.
- Taking customer details on clipboards when a customer drops off their car.
- Washing the cars with squirters and sponges
- Squeezing out sponges and cloths
- Repairing the cars with tools.
- Working in the office area – taking phone bookings or payments for repairs.

The ultimate guide to mark making in the early years

Developing dexterity

Developing very fine small motor skills will help your children form letters correctly. These activities require a high level of focus and attention, so that the child's brain forms the connections required to make the hand move in a certain way and to a certain place. The following activities all help increase children's dexterity:

- Tearing up paper.

- Cutting up paper with a pair of scissors.

- Threading with beads.

- Using tweezers to pick up small items.

- Using chopsticks, for instance to pick up noodles.

- Writing with feathers dipped in paint or ink.

- Doing up buttons and zips.

- Putting shoes on independently.

- Using hole and paper punches.

- Using staplers.

- Putting paper clips on paper (far trickier than you'd imagine).

- Playing with wind-up toys.

- Using sticky tape or masking tape to make pictures, wrap things up, or join things together.

activity

HAPPY BIRTHDAY TO YOU!

YOU WILL NEED

- A variety of different sized boxes
- Sticky tape, preferably in child-friendly dispensers
- Several pairs of scissors
- A selection of wrapping paper
- A selection of string, ribbons and other decorative items
- Birthday cards and envelopes

LEARNING INTENTIONS

- To help the children develop their dexterity and fine motor skills
- To practise using a pair of scissors to cut accurately
- To write for a purpose

INSTRUCTIONS

This activity is great for encouraging children to use their fingers and develop their dexterity. Get your children to wrap presents and write cards for a real person (mum, dad, a friend) or a story character's birthday. Offer a selection of different kinds of boxes, pre-cut paper, rolls of wrapping paper and ribbons, as well as different birthday cards and envelopes.

The ultimate guide to mark making in the early years

Moving individual fingers

As well as activities where the children are required to 'pinch' their fingers together, encourage your children to learn how to move their fingers separately as well. You can do this by:

- Using songs such as 'Ten Little Fishes' where the children must make their fingers hide or disappear. (Find a link which gives lots of examples of number songs in the companion website.) [website]

- Using finger and hand puppets, for instance to retell a story.

- Playing on a keyboard or piano.

- Making shadow puppets using fingers and torches within a darkened tent.

- Making drawings in different substances (mud, sand, paint) using their fingertips, particularly the index finger.

Eye to hand coordination

When we write our eyes must guide our hands to form the correct letter shapes, to stay on the line and within the page. Eye tracking skills are also vital for reading, so that the child can fix on and follow text along a page. This skill is sometimes referred to as eye to body coordination or, more technically, as 'visual-motor integration'. Success in many sports is based around good eye/hand coordination – tennis being a prime example.

Use gross motor activities to build strength and coordination, giving children large resources to begin with (a large bat, a large ball, a big target). Gradually work with smaller and smaller resources, as the children become more accurate in their eye to hand/arm coordination. Incorporate plenty of opportunities for fine motor activities that build fine eye/hand coordination as well. You can find lots of ideas opposite to develop this area.

Gross motor activities for eye/hand coordination

- Playing catch with a ball in groups or with partners.

- Hitting a ball with a bat.

- Tossing a bean bag in the air and catching it.

- With children standing in a row, getting them to pass a ball over their heads or through their legs.

- Encouraging the children to follow an object with their eyes, for instance when programming remote control toys such as a Bee-Bot®.

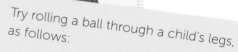

Try rolling a ball through a child's legs, as follows:

- Get the child to stand with his back to you, legs apart in a V shape.

- Now roll a small ball through his legs.

- As soon as he sees it appear, he must follow it with his eyes and then move to collect it.

Fine motor activities for eye/hand coordination

- Building towers with blocks.

- Putting pegs into a peg board.

- Threading beads onto a string.

- Cutting up food for snack time.

- Colouring in.

- Icing biscuits.

- Placing Hama beads into a design on a peg board (for dexterous older children).

- Playing a xylophone.

- Cutting or tearing paper, especially around an outline.

- Tracing between two lines, or through a maze, with a finger or pencil.

BALLOON 'KEEPY UPPY'

YOU WILL NEED

- Balloons – at least one per child (have a few spares in case some pop)

- An open space – indoors is best as the wind makes this tricky outside

LEARNING INTENTIONS

- To build eye to hand coordination in a fun, safe way

- To develop counting skills

INSTRUCTIONS

Give each of your children a balloon. Explain that they must keep it up in the air for as long as possible by tapping it upwards with their hands. You could do this as a group, counting upwards as you go, or it could be done individually.

Set a challenge for the children to increase the number of keepy uppys they do over a series of days or weeks, as their eye to hand coordination improves. They could write how many they managed on the balloon, to take home with them.

Vision and eye/hand coordination

It stands to reason that, in order to coordinate the eyes to the hand or body, children need to have good vision. While an eye test checks for clarity of vision, there are various other issues which may affect a child's ability to work with marks on a page. They include:

Eye teaming problems: this is where the child's eyes find it hard to aim at the same point on the page. When the brain reads the information coming from each eye it creates a blurred image. The child has to strain to stop the print from blurring.

Tracking problems: to follow marks on a page, children must learn to track them. Children who have tracking problems struggle to control their eye movements at close range.

Focus problems: school frequently requires children to focus at a distance (look at the board) and then change to focusing up close (write on the page). Children who have focus problems may suffer from headaches when asked to change focus frequently.

Vision perception problems: these are a variety of issues with giving meaning to what is seen, i.e. to perceiving marks on a page. For instance visual spatial orientation is about being able to perceive where your body is in relation to the world around you.

(website) Visit the companion website for a link to a useful website on this subject. If you have concerns about a child you work with, you will find a very helpful checklist of the symptoms of vision problems on this site.

Holding a mark making tool

A key part of what makes us human is the fact that we can use a mark making tool to communicate with each other via written symbols. The skill of holding and manoeuvring the tool takes time to develop – at first we just make scribbles, but gradually the letter shapes start to take form. By making it seem fun and natural to work with different mark making tools, you give your children the chance to build up the skills that they need to be able to write.

The role of drawing and painting

Drawing and painting are forms of 'mark making', which will help the child shape letters when they are introduced. (As well as, of course, being a skill and an art form in its own right.) At first, children do not differentiate between marks made to create a picture and marks made to convey meaning through words. Gradually, though, they learn to separate out their drawing from their 'writing'. Often, the first 'word' that they attempt to write spontaneously will be their own name.

Most young children love to get messy when painting, and this is a key reason why it is so important to offer it as a part of a child's preschool, nursery or primary school experience. Parents may shy away from doing painting at home because of the mess that can result. In the early years environment, we don't mind when children cover their hands with paints to make hand prints or if they get more paint on them than on the paper. Painting offers huge rewards in terms of sensory experiences and the chance for creative expression. It also helps children develop many of the skills they need to hold and manipulate a mark making tool. For some fun ways to work with paint:

- Dip marbles in paint, then roll them around on paper to see what marks they make.

- Tread the feet of toy dinosaurs in paint, to use as stampers, and create trails of 'dinosaur footprints' across the page.

- Get the children to tread in paint, and then make footprints across a long roll of paper.

- Use paint with natural materials, for instance leaves, sticks or the stems of long grasses.

Talking about drawing

Children often create a narrative as they draw or paint a picture, talking through what they are creating. Encourage your children to use drawing and painting alongside verbal expression – this extends their vocabulary and helps them understand narrative structure. Avoid imposing your own interpretation on a child's drawing – if you ask 'is that a dinosaur?' the child may just agree. You might have noticed that often, marks appear within young children's drawings and paintings that look similar to letters. Gradually, the children understand that marks can hold meaning in the form of a word and start to experiment with them.

Learning the correct grasp

Although the eventual aim for handwriting is for children to develop a tripod grip, it is tricky for small hands to achieve this. Children of 3 years and under tend to use a fist grip. This fist grip usually develops into a finger grasp, perhaps using all five fingers.

Depending on the size, strength and ability of the individual child, they should be ready to start using a correct pencil grasp from the age of 3 or 4 years old. As the child reaches school age, and is expected to write more frequently, it's particularly important to discourage incorrect grip. Once a poor habit takes hold it is hard to break: even if it does not appear to disadvantage the child at present, it may cause difficulties with writing later on in the child's school career. Keep a close eye on your children as they become more confident about holding a pencil and start to form letters. If you notice incorrect habits forming, for instance a child who continues to use a fist grip, intervene before the habit becomes ingrained. Chunky pencil grips can help a child who is struggling to hold a pencil correctly.

The ideal is for children to develop a form of what is known as a 'dynamic tripod grasp' (sometimes also called the 'dynamic tripod grip'). With this grip:

- The pen or pencil is held between the thumb and the index and middle fingers.

- The child makes a 'tripod' shape with the thumb and fingers.

- The fingers, rather than the wrist, move the pencil.

- The hand and fingers are relaxed and a light pressure is exerted on the paper.

- The pen or pencil rests comfortably on the web space between the thumb and index finger.

- The fingers and thumb form a 'C' shape, rather than the space being flattened out.

- The pencil is held with the tips of the thumb/fingers rather than in the joint of the thumb.

However, each child will develop his or her own particular style of 'tripod' grip, as you can see in the photos.

activity

THE PEN OLYMPICS

YOU WILL NEED

- A child, group of children or whole class
- A pencil for each child
- A pair of chopsticks for each child
- A pile of small objects, for instance paper clips or beads
- A pot for each child

LEARNING INTENTIONS

- To help the children develop their finger strength and dexterity
- To check for grip weaknesses in individuals

INSTRUCTIONS

Host the 'Pencil Olympics' with your children, to strengthen fingers and to check issues with pencil grips. These activities could be done individually, or as a whole class warm-up for writing.

Event One: Hold the pencil using a dynamic tripod grasp. Now, they must move the pencil through their fingers until they are holding it by the end, then go back along the pencil to the tip.

Event Two: Hold the pencil between the index and middle fingers and twirl the 'baton' around and around, just using the tips of the fingers.

Event Three: Hold a pair of chopsticks with a dynamic tripod grasp. Now, pick up the small objects as quickly as possible and place them in the pots using the chopsticks.

Supporting children who are left-handed

Hand preference tends to be fixed after about 3 years of age; between 8 and 15 per cent of the world's population will have a preference for using their left hand. Very few people are genuinely ambidextrous, although some people may use different hands for different activities. For those children whose preference is to use their left hand, this has the potential to cause them difficulties, particularly when it comes to mark making and writing. You need to be aware of the issues which may arise, and work to pre-empt and overcome them. This might be through the resources that you offer, or through the way that you set up activities.

A child who is left-handed will have to push the writing tool across the page, rather than pulling it as a right hander does. The child will also cover the marks as they move along the line, potentially smudging the writing and also making it harder to retain the sense of what has been written. Some people who are left-handed develop a kind of 'hooked' posture, whereby they hook their hand over their writing (so that they can see what they are doing as they write). However, by helping the child adopt the correct posture and writing position when they first learn to write, you can avoid this.

Here are some top tips for supporting children who are left-handed:

- Present mark making activities at the child's midline, rather than to one side – this will help children decide on hand preference for themselves.

- It is easier for left-handed children to write on a slope, so offer them an easel or a raised surface.

- It is also a very good idea to give left-handed children chances to do large-scale mark making, so that they don't always feel that their hand is getting in the way of what they want to write or draw.

- Advise a child who is left-handed to hold the pencil below the writing as they write, so that they can see what they are doing.

- Encourage the child to tilt the paper at 45 degrees clockwise, so that the top of the page tilts slightly down to the right.

- Demonstrate how to hold the pencil at about 2.5 to 3.8 cm away from the tip to help the child see what they are writing.

- Watch the child to make sure they do not begin to adopt an awkward posture.

- Minimise pressure on the child to write 'neatly' at first, as this might lead them to use excessive grip pressure in an effort to make neat marks.

- Watch where you sit the child – make sure they are to the left of any right-handers, so that the children do not bump elbows as they write.

- When left-handed children learn letter formation, remember that it is fine to slope letters to the left, as well as to the right. (If you are right-handed, you may need to overcome your instinctive feeling that this is 'wrong'.)

- Remember that letter formation is slightly different for left-handed children (see the companion website for more information). website

Check whether you have left-handed scissors on offer in your setting and offer these to your left-handed children, to see if they would prefer to use them. With a left-handed pair of scissors, the left blade is kept on top, so that the children can see where they are cutting as the pair of scissors moves through the paper.

The ultimate guide to mark making in the early years

Mirror writing

Some famous left-handed people have used mirror writing, for instance Leonardo da Vinci wrote most of his personal notes in this way. If you notice that a child is starting to write his letters backwards and back to front, encourage him to start writing from the left hand side of the page. Tracing over words (with arrows to indicate direction) can also be a helpful strategy to overcome this problem. See the companion website for a link to a very useful site all about 'handedness', and which gives advice on how to teach children who are left-handed to write. You can also find a link to a site that gives left-handed letter formation instructions. **website**

Mark making and posture

In order to control our writing, we must first be able to control our bodies. Those children who do not have good core strength find it harder to write neatly. Indeed, they may find it hard to sit at a seat with good posture for any length of time. Watch out for the telltale signs of poorly developed core muscles – these are the children who:

- Slump or flop over onto the table when they are writing.
- Lean with their stomachs against the table.
- Use their elbows to support their bodies.
- Wrap their legs around the chair or table to gain balance.
- Walk with their tummies sticking out, rather than their tails 'tucked under'.

These children will need your support to build up their gross motor strength before they can hope to hold the correct posture for writing. Doing more writing sitting badly at a table is not a solution to help them develop the necessary muscular control.

Correct posture for writing

Your children will spend a good proportion of the next ten to fifteen years of their lives writing, sat at desks. It's therefore vital that they learn to sit properly. An incorrect posture may lead to an incorrect pencil grasp, and also to back and neck pain. If you stop for a moment and think about your own posture when you write, you will probably be aware that you have picked up some bad habits over time. (As I type this my legs are crossed and my back is slumped, although I do at least have an adjustable chair and my elbows are at the correct angle to the table.)

The ideal is for children to develop what is known as the '90–90–90' position: in other words, a body shape with three 90 degree angles:

- Feet flat on floor with a 90 degree angle at the ankles.
- Knees bent at 90 degrees.
- Arms flat on the table with a 90 degree angle at the elbows.

Where possible, ensure that the chair is the correct height in relation to the table, so that the lower arms are not tilted up or down and the elbows are roughly in line with the waist. Typically, the furniture in schools does not adjust to children of different ages and heights. You might need to offer cushions for small children to raise themselves up, or, if possible, tables at a variety of heights.

Part 3

I can concentrate, focus and behave

In this section

- Help your children develop control of their impulses

- Encourage your children to make good choices about learning

- Develop effective rules and structures for behaviour

- Help your children build focus and pay attention for longer periods of time

- Understand the link between concentration and attainment in writing

Consider this...

Success at writing is inextricably linked to behaviour; if a child cannot stay in a seat, focus on the task or have the patience to practise and persevere it is inevitable that their writing will be poor. Children need to learn to listen, to focus, to pay attention and to be self-disciplined if they are to get the best out of education. So much of school relies on the ability to use language – to read, to write, to discuss. And where a child cannot use language effectively, school becomes a daily trial by literacy. Indeed, children will sometimes turn to misbehaviour simply *because* their weak language skills mean they cannot access learning. It feels better to hide that fact from their peers by becoming the class clown, than to admit to it.

In the early years of their lives, children have short concentration spans. As someone once memorably said to me, teaching preschoolers is 'like herding cats'. This is part of the reason why a child-initiated approach to learning makes sense for preschool-aged children – they focus on something that holds their interest, but can find it much harder to focus on something that the adult insists they do. Gradually, young children learn how to concentrate for longer and longer periods of time, and on a wider range of activities – including some they might not particularly enjoy. Learning how to do this is much harder for some than for others. Concentration, focus and self-regulation all play a crucial part in a child's mark making and writing and it is therefore vital that we support the development of these skills.

Impulse control and self-regulation

Babies and young children typically have poor impulse control – they find it hard or impossible to think before they say or do something. As we grow older we learn to control our initial emotional responses to a situation and to replace that with a more rational and considered reaction. In other words, we learn self-discipline. Even as an adult, however, this is often not easy to do when you are faced with a difficult situation or if you are tired and stressed. A very young child:

- Wants their needs met immediately.

- Doesn't understand why sometimes this cannot happen.

- May use emotional outbursts as a way of communicating.

- May shout or lash out if their desires are frustrated.

- Is prone to being affected by physical issues such as hunger, tiredness and so on.

You may have noticed how some children in your early years setting will:

- Snatch toys or resources off someone else without asking.

- Call out the answers when you ask a question of the whole group.

- Push to the front of the queue.

- Throw a tantrum if they don't get what they want.

- Shout to try and get what they want.

These are the children who have poor impulse control.

The ultimate guide to mark making in the early years

Developing impulse control

A key part of your role when working with young children is to help them learn how to control or refocus their impulses. This important aspect of learning helps us function within wider society. We cannot simply scream and throw things and lash out if we do not get what we want. Preschools, nurseries and schools are a miniature version of society – a community of people working together for the best interests of all.

A good example of why impulse control is so important within education is the child's ability (or inability) to sit on the carpet and raise a hand. You might have noticed how some children will always call out, and it takes you a long time to break this habit, if you ever manage to do so. You can help your children develop impulse control by:

* Playing games and doing activities that rely on taking turns.

* Talking about why it's important to share.

* Boosting empathy by talking about emotions in relation to behaviour – how does it feel when someone snatches a toy off you?

* Ignoring any outbursts or tantrums, unless the child is in immediate danger.

* Structuring your day so that the children do not get too tired, over excited or bored, so that there is less reason for them to lash out.

* Gradually increasing the time that the children spend on those activities requiring greater levels of self-discipline.

* Making sure not to pay attention to misbehaviour, but to focus on those behaving well instead.

* Breaking the 'habit' of calling out, by ignoring children who shout out answers and only asking those who have their hands raised.

* Giving angry children an outlet for their frustrations, for instance a cushion in a soft area to hit if they need to let off steam.

When you work with children, you also need to control your *own* impulses in order to better manage behaviour. This is tricky because teaching can be stressful, noisy, messy, hard work. The impulses you need to control include the impulse to:

• Snap at children when they don't do what you want, or if they misbehave.	• Focus far more of your attention on the 'difficult' children than on the 'easy' ones.
• Raise your voice or shout when you're feeling tired or stressed.	• Pay attention to poor behaviour, rather than highlighting examples of the behaviour you want.

When dealing with problem behaviour, a good rule of thumb is that you usually don't need to make an immediate intervention unless someone is likely to get hurt, or is hurting others.

Talking about choices

Young children can find it hard to make sensible decisions and good choices, and to understand why they can't always have exactly what they want. When we are very young, we don't know much about how the world works, or what is good for us. This might be about day-to-day routines ('Why *can't* I wear my princess dress when it's snowing?'; 'Why *can't* I eat chocolate for dinner every day?') or about behaviour ('Why *should* I have to sit on the carpet if I don't want to?') Again, this is all tied up with learning impulse control.

Use simple choices to help your children learn to make good decisions. As they get older, and understand more about their world, these choices can become more complex. Being able to make good decisions is important for learning how to behave, but also for learning how to create an effective piece of writing.

Your choices might be very simple ones, for instance about your daily routine:

> *'Do you want milk or water?'*

Or they could be choices around behaviour:

> *'You have a choice. You can play nicely with this toy instead of banging it on the floor. Or, I will need to take the toy away so that it doesn't get broken.'*

Behaviour, listening and noise

Individual writing works best when it is done in a silent, or near silent, working atmosphere, because it is easier to concentrate and hear your inner 'writing voice'. Some people enjoy music in the background when they write, while others find it distracting. You (and your children) need to learn how to control the noise levels within the classroom or setting as a whole, for times when quiet or silence is required to write. This can prove tricky with young children, particularly during continuous provision.

When you need silent attention, much of your success will be to do with the clarity of your expectation, how you present the challenge and the confidence you project when you explain what you need. Consider the difference between:

> *'Come on children, could we have a bit of quiet, ssh, ssh, ssh. Look, please be quiet, you're really giving me a headache.'*

And a clearer, more direct and confident approach:

> *'Right! [claps hands] Eyes on me, please. When I say 'go', I'm going to challenge you to be completely silent for a 2 minutes. Do you think you can manage that? Of course you can! Three, two, one ... go!'*

The ultimate guide to mark making in the early years

Rules about listening and noise

Think carefully about the rules you create around speaking and listening. Consider the messages you send to the children. If your rule is 'We speak quietly', does this always apply? Are there situations or times (outdoors, during singing, in Physical Education (PE)) that the rule is not appropriate? At our preschool our rule is, *'We use our inside voices inside'* to help the children understand situation-appropriate behaviour.

It can work well to get the class to practise speaking at different volume levels. By controlling their own sound levels, they become more conscious about how loud they are speaking, and how well they are listening. You could use 'silent zone' for listening to someone else talking, 'paired voice' for conversations between friends, 'activity voice' for physical activity and 'outdoor voice' for your outdoor areas.

When working on expectations:

- Use plenty of repetition to ensure that golden rules are understood.

- Practise following the rules, for instance getting the class to talk at 'paired voice' level, then at 'activity voice' level.

- Model the rules at all times for your children.

- Use non-verbal cues and pauses to encourage better listening, rather than constantly asking for quiet.

- Create visual representations of your rules so that the children can refer to them.

- Have a 'focus of the day' or 'focus of the week', rather than trying to get the children to retain lots of rules at once.

Too much noise?

If you frequently find that your setting gets too loud, and it feels like the children are not very good at listening to each other, consider whether your set-up is contributing to the problem. Constant noise can be stressful for both young children and adults and it can certainly distract from a focus on writing. The questions below should help guide your thinking:

- Is there one area of the room where most of the noise happens?

- What kind of activities tend to lead to lots of noise?

- Am I achieving a good balance of activities in the room – some loud, others quieter?

- Do the adults model good listening and reasonable noise levels?

- Are the children getting regular reminders to control the overall noise?

- Are these reminders visual as well as verbal?

- Is there a gender divide when it comes to noise – is one group (boys/girls) louder than the other?

- If yes, why is this? Do we appear to have different expectations of the children's behaviour and noise levels, depending on whether they are boys or girls?

- Are there places where the children can go to have some quiet time?

- Are there times during the day when the whole class or whole group gets some quiet time?

It can work well to make a visual representation of how noisy the group is, to encourage the children to control the overall noise levels. For instance:

- A 'noise-o-meter' with a moveable dial – basically a box with a dial fixed on it. Ask your children what level the noise-o-meter should be set at for each activity.

- A 'noise levels graph' drawn on your board.

- A 'traffic lights' noise meter, downloaded onto your interactive whiteboard.

Consider using a variety of sounds and other signals to get the children's attention, particularly during continuous provision or when the overall noise levels are high. You might use a bell, a raised hand, a series of claps or a 'join in with me' activity such as 'Simon Says'.

Learning to hold my focus

Writing requires focus – the ability to concentrate on one thing for an extended period of time. Fortunately, concentration and focus are skills that we can help our children develop. You might have noticed that some of your children already have high levels of focus when they join you, while others barely seem able to sustain attention on one thing for more than a few seconds. Some will sit enchanted by a single object or activity, spending ages playing with it or studying it. Others will flit from activity to activity, or play with a toy for only moments before discarding it.

Those who lack the ability to pay attention can struggle when they move into the more formal school years. The requirement to 'stay in your seat' can be a real challenge for children with poor focus. A lack of focus/attention might be due to:

- An excessive amount of 'screen time' at an early age.

- A lack of stimulation – limited exposure to experiences outside the home, to play or to undivided adult attention.

- Over stimulation – being in an environment which is excessively noisy or full of distractions.

- Some kinds of SEND, such as attention deficit hyperactivity disorder (ADHD).

Keep an eye out for those children who really struggle to maintain their focus, or to make eye contact with others. If you notice a child who constantly 'flits' from activity to activity, and who finds it very difficult to sit still, flag up your concerns with your Special Educational Needs and Disabilities Coordinator (SENDCo) early on.

A rough but useful rule of thumb for children's concentration spans is their age, plus two. When working with young children, you only really have about 5 to 10 minutes in which they can concentrate with full focus. What you might have noticed is that, when they have chosen the activity for themselves, your children will typically be able to focus on it for longer.

Using focus activities

Help your children develop their focus by doing activities specifically designed to build concentration – those activities where they focus on one thing for an extended period of time. Here are some suggestions:

- Ask the children to close their eyes and focus on listening. What can they hear around them? Can they hear anything outside the room? Encourage them to sit with their eyes closed, listening, for gradually extended periods of time. This is almost like a form of meditation and children typically find it relaxing.

- Repeat the listening exercise, but this time instead of asking the children to listen for sounds, encourage them to visualise a story in their heads. You can 'tell' a story ('you are in the woods, look around you, you notice a tower, you walk towards it'). Alternatively, you can encourage the children to visualise a positive image of their own ('you are somewhere warm and comfy, look around and see where you are, what can you see, hear, touch?').

- Get the children to stand in an open space, such as a hall or playground. Explain that you are going to play 'Walk and Freeze'. The children should walk freely around the room, without banging into each other. When they hear you bang a drum, they should freeze completely. When they hear you bang the drum again, they can start walking again. Repeat several times, until everyone can stop and start at the same moment.

- Ask the children to sit or stand opposite a partner, to do a paired focus activity. Ask them to imagine they are looking in a mirror. When one child moves, the other child should mirror their movements exactly. You might like to demonstrate first, using a mirror, to show them how the opposite hand appears to move when we look at a reflection.

- Do a circle ball throw with your group. Stand the children in a circle. Explain that you are going to throw a large ball across the circle. You will make eye contact with the child before you throw the ball, so that they know it is coming to them. Each time they are about to throw the ball, the child should make eye contact with the person it will be thrown to.

- 'Statues' is a great personal favourite for calming a group down, and for encouraging focus (you might also know it by the name 'Sleeping Lions'). Ask the children to get into a comfy position. Explain that, when you say 'go', they are going to freeze as still as statues. They must keep their hands, feet and eyes still, although they are allowed to breathe. At first, you may find that younger children struggle to stay still at all. Build up the time gradually.

Mucky focus: being absorbed

The ability to become absorbed in something, to the exclusion of all else, is something that you might have noticed in even the youngest of children. In fact, often young children are more able than adults to fall into a focus – whether in an imaginative world, or a purely earthbound one. This is sometimes called a 'working meditation' – it is the kind of 'in the zone' mental state you achieve when you're doing something that you really enjoy. Hours pass while seeming like minutes.

This absorption and focus are essential for learning to write, and for sticking at writing when you are doing it. In the early years it often happens when the child is involved in a particularly mucky and multisensory experience. Because all of the senses are involved this seems to 'hook' a child in. There's the added bonus that sensory play is often great for fine motor control – learning to really feel objects through your fingers, and consequently to feel and manipulate a writing tool. Mucky play happens most easily outdoors, using natural materials. I can remember my own child being fascinated by mud and spending hours out in the garden pouring water onto soil and getting toy diggers 'stuck' in it. Throughout this play, children are learning how to focus, how to use their hands and fingers and also how the world around them works.

I remember watching one of our preschoolers completely engrossed in scooping out the squishy insides of a pumpkin to make a Halloween lantern. From time to time the child would extract a small piece of pumpkin, hold it to her nose, sniff it, frown a bit, give it a little lick and then put it to one side. The focus and concentration in what she was doing was extraordinary.

Mucky activities

You can offer mucky activities just for child-initiated exploration (playing with water and soil) and others with a specific purpose (finding bugs that are hidden in the ground and counting them). Some parents are resistant to the idea of children getting covered in gloop or mud. If this is the case you might:

- Have a dedicated 'mucky day' and ask parents to send in their children in old clothes.

- Put regular reminders in a parent newsletter explaining how important messy play is, and how it will take place regularly at your setting.

- Buy a set of waterproof, washable, outdoor overalls for the children to wear.

- Run a 'mucky play' workshop, to help parents understand how valuable this kind of exploration is.

Use these mucky activities to get your children absorbed and learning how to focus. These activities are all great for fine motor skills as well.

When it snows, gather some snow to take indoors, so that the children can get hands-on with it.

Make creepy crawly jelly. Set plastic insects in jelly, for the children to dig out.

Make corn flour gloop. Slowly add one cup of cold water to two cups of corn flour in a bowl. This makes a lovely, sensory gloop mixture for the children to play with.

Put cooked spaghetti in your water tray for the children to handle. Offer tools such as chopsticks for them to use to pick up the strands. Add a bit of washing up liquid to keep the pasta slippery.

Fill a plastic book tray with water and objects around a theme: different leaves and natural materials work well. Freeze the tray overnight in your freezer. Now put this out in your water tray or tuff tray, so that the children can experiment with how ice feels and how it melts. The children love waiting for the objects to be released from the block.

Mix up Gelli Baff® for your water tray, putting different toys related to a particular theme in it for the children to play with.

Put soapy water into a tuff spot, along with a plastic hula hoop. Get your children to stand in the middle then slowly pull up the hoop. With luck they will be standing in a giant bubble!

Create papier mâché masks, using newspaper and water-based glue. First, blow up a balloon and cover this with torn up strips of newspaper soaked in glue, in layers. Do this over several days and leave to dry thoroughly. Cut the balloon in half to make two mask shapes, then cut holes for the eyes and mouth, decorate and add elastic.

Make porridge for mucky play around a *Goldilocks and the Three Bears* theme.

Part 4

I understand that marks hold meaning

In this section

- Explore how children convey meaning through their marks

- Help your children acquire the concepts needed for writing

- Examine how children learn to write their names

- Explore the role of shapes and symbols within writing

- Learn how stories enhance your children's conceptual development

- Find fascinating ways to use non-fiction texts in your setting

Consider this...

Letters and words are a series of shapes and symbols. In most languages these shapes correlate to the sounds we make within speech. We can sound out the phonemes (blocks of letter sound) in a word to read it. We can use our knowledge of these sounds to write the word and gain meaning from it or to use it to convey meaning to others. A key developmental step for young children is to understand that different shapes, and combinations of shapes, equate to different letters and therefore different sounds within the English language. This is a key step in learning to read – blending together individual phonemes helps the child make sense of what the words say.

Sharing stories is perhaps the most important way in which we show young children that marks on a page hold both sound and meaning. If a child is read to every day from a young age, this reinforces the notion that books and print are an important part of culture and society. The child also starts to learn that books work in a particular way – that in English they are read from front to back, from the left-hand side of the page to the right-hand side and from the top of the page to the bottom. When the children come to read and write stories, they will mirror the book behaviours learned in the early years from parents or carers and from you.

As well as understanding that marks hold meaning, children also begin to show their patterns of thinking through marks. Before they are even able to form letters, you will see them making meaning through symbols and other related marks that might look something like letters or numbers. Look closely at a child's pictures and you can gain a sense of how they see the world.

Mark making and schemas

Mark making helps young children make sense of their world, and express their thinking to others. The patterns of marks that you observe can help you understand their thought, even before they can express what they mean. You may be used to observing children's schemas: those regular patterns of play identified by Piaget, which help children organise knowledge and relate to the world. For instance:

- A transportation schema: a child who enjoys moving blocks and toys from one place to another, and who loves filling up bags.

- An enclosure schema: a child who often fills up containers, or who loves to climb inside boxes.

- A transformation schema: a child who loves to turn one thing into something else, for instance adding paint to the sand.

Often, these patterns of thought will also be apparent in young children's mark making. For instance some children are fascinated by a specific object/animal – every mark becomes a representation of that thing. Similarly, young children's earliest mark making will often feature images of people. In the piece here, drawn by a three-year-old, you can see definite signs of faces, and perhaps some shapes meant to denote letters as well. Children try to make meaning with their writing, right from the earliest moments.

Signs and symbols

We are surrounded by signs and symbols. They convey simple meanings quickly and forcefully – this is why they are so widely used in branding and advertising. Well before they can read text, children understand what many symbols mean. Show your children the golden 'M' symbol used by McDonalds, or the tick used by Nike. You may be surprised at how many of your children can instantly say what these symbols refer to.

The visual nature of symbols means they are easily understood, even by young children, and this makes symbols and graphic pictures perfect for conveying meanings in your setting. You can use symbols and signs to help the children understand your routines and structures, and also to learn about communicating meaning through marks. Symbols are also particularly useful for children who have EAL or those with particular kinds of SEND. You could create:

- A visual register using various signs and/or symbols. For instance, the children could put their name on the 'sad' or 'happy' side of a board, or under a picture of the drink they would like at snack time.

- Visual timetables for the whole group or for individuals, with images showing what happens at different times of the day.

- Labels within areas in your setting, for instance a 'Germ Busters' sign in the toilets.

- Symbols for each of your golden rules, to back up discussion about what the rules mean.

- Stickers with a 'thumbs up' symbol on them, to give to children as a reward.

activity

STOP, GO, NO ENTRY!

YOU WILL NEED

- Poles or mop/broom handles
- Large pieces of cardboard
- A pair of scissors
- Paints or felt tip pens
- Gaffer tape or heavy duty parcel tape
- Ride-on toys
- Outdoor chalks

LEARNING INTENTIONS

- To examine how shapes and symbols have different meanings
- To use these symbols within an imaginative context
- To make marks on different surfaces

INSTRUCTIONS

Although you can buy ready-made road signs, it's far more fun and valuable to get your children to make some of their own. You might choose No Entry (a red circle with a white line across), Stop (a red octagon with STOP written in white), Mini Roundabout (a blue circle with three arrows going round) or perhaps some speed limits (written with black numbers on a white circle, with a red line around it).

Show the children a variety of signs and symbols, and talk about what these mean. Discuss the different colours that are used. Why do they think red is chosen for signs that give an order or a limit? You might also go for a walk around your local area, with a digital camera, so that the children can take photos of different signs. Now explain that you are going to create a road system for the ride-on toys, with signs to show directions, speed limits and so on.

Create your signs by painting the cardboard shapes and then attaching them to the poles. Get the children to draw a series of roads on the ground, using outdoor chalks. They can then experiment with driving their cars and other vehicles around the roads, following the instructions on the signs.

Visit the companion website for a link to a site that offers downloadable PDFs of different types of road signs.

`website`

Me and my name

Our names are a crucial part of who we are. They give us a sense of identity, attachment and belonging. Right from the earliest moments of our lives we hear our names over and over, most often being spoken by the people that we love. Using marks to write their own name is one of the first pieces of writing that many children try to do – saying, in effect, 'this is me'! Just think of the graffiti that has existed from ancient times. The urge to mark our name on public surfaces is a very strong one indeed.

There are plenty of ways you can motivate your children to learn the shape and letters of their name, and to make marks to write it:

- Get your children to self-register using their name. At our setting we use name labels with self fasteners on the back kept in a tray. Parents are encouraged to help their child find their own name and stick it onto the registration board. By seeing and picking out their names every day, the children become used to seeing the shape and identifying it as theirs.

- Put children's names on their pegs and book trays. Include a picture beside the name which remains consistent every time the child's name is used. You can link the initial sound of the image to the child's name, for instance a 'Train' for 'Tomek', to help him learn that first sound/letter in his name.

- As the children get older, and start to recognise their names, remove the picture from beside the name so that they identify the actual word.

- Later on, encourage them to replace the adult written name tags with ones they have written themselves.

- When children draw or paint a picture, or make a model, encourage them to participate in writing their name on it.

- Write name labels in other situations for instance, when planting and growing sunflowers.

- Offer the children a laminated copy of their name, with arrows to show them which way to write the letters. We offer opportunities for our older children to practise tracing over their names. It's important to have close adult supervision when they do this, to ensure that they are forming the letters correctly.

The ultimate guide to mark making in the early years

You can also use creative activities to encourage the children to become familiar with their names. They could:

- Make their name out of twigs.

- Shape and bake the letters of their name using dough.

- Ice cakes with the initial letter of their name.

- Use magazine cut outs/collage techniques to make their name.

- Write their names using silver or gold pens, on black paper.

Dealing with parental pressure to write names

Parents are often especially keen to see their children writing their names as it seems like a logical first step in 'learning to write'. At our setting, at times we have experienced pressure from some parents for us to sit their children down, and insist that they trace over their names until they learn to write them. We've also had some children who have been taught to write their names at home, through repeated practice (and sometimes in capital letters!). Of course, there's no reason why parents should know how early writing develops. Equally, some parents will have gone to school at a time when teaching was done in a more formal way. It's important to communicate information to parents about this part of early child development. You might:

- Use leaflets, parent workshops and 'hands on' sessions to explain about the best approaches to develop early mark making.

- Help parents understand that it is can be counterproductive to get very young children to write their names 'properly'. If children do not have the finger strength to form the letters correctly, they can get into bad habits around letter formation or pencil grip. These habits then have to be broken later on.

- While most small children are keen to write their names, it can be off putting for young children to see 'writing my name' as an enforced task, and this might even put them off wanting to write.

- For older children, who have developed sufficient pre-writing skills, offer concerned parents a laminated guide showing how the child should form the letters of their names correctly.

Children come to writing their name at different times, but it is very rare indeed (even for children with special needs) that they never learn to write it at all. In the image below you can see how the process of a child learning to write their name develops over the course of several years:

1. First marks made at **age two** – a sample from a postcard written by Edite which she told us said 'Edite is going to Portugal'.

2. **Age three**: We can start to see the first clear letter shapes beginning to emerge.

3. **Age three and a half**: Edite's name is starting to become more recognizable.

4. **Age four**: In the term before starting school, the writing is wobbly but easy to read – she had been practising tracing over her name.

5. and 6. **Age four and five** in Reception: Notice how the letter 'e' is hard for her to write at first, but by the end of the year all the letters are correctly formed.

7. and 8. **Age five and rising six** in Year 1: Edite can now print neatly, and has just learned cursive writing, so is keen to practise joining up.

The ultimate guide to mark making in the early years

GRAFFITI WALL (only for the brave!)

YOU WILL NEED

- A flat area of wall in your outdoor area
- Alternatively, an outdoor chalkboard, or chalkboard paint
- Outdoor chalks
- Paint or large marker pens (if you're allowed a permanent wall)
- Outdoor chalks

LEARNING INTENTIONS

- To encourage children to write, including their names
- To show writing as an act of public expression

INSTRUCTIONS

There's something peculiarly enthralling for children about writing on a wall (particularly where that writing is permanent). You might get them to mark make directly onto a brick wall. Alternatively, you could fix up a chalkboard, or paint a section of wall, fence or the side of a shed with chalkboard paint.

If you have an understanding head teacher or setting leader, why not suggest the idea of a permanent graffiti wall for the children? This is simply a wall that is designated for public art/writing using permanent writing tools. It can be painted over several times a year, as it gets full of marks. Your graffiti wall could be a section of wall indoors or an area outside. Make it clear to the children that it is *only* this section of wall on which they can make their marks. For older children with a better grasp of written language, set rules about the kind of language they can use, and also about not making personal comments about other children.

Alternatively, you can always cover a section of wall, or the top of a table, with lining paper. Or you could buy some wooden tables and chairs for the children to decorate – it's essentially the same thing.

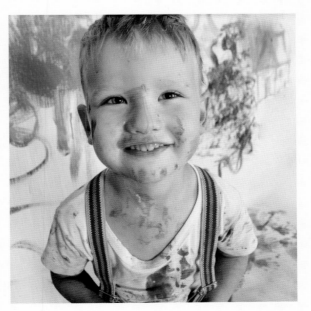

Seeing shapes

a b c d e f g h i j k l m n o p q r s t u v w x y z

If you stop for a moment and look at the alphabet as it's written above, you will start to notice that each letter is made up of a distinctive set of shapes. There are circles and part circles, in the letters 'a', 'b', 'c' and 'o', among others. There are vertical lines, for instance in the letters 'b', 'l' and 't'. There are horizontal lines, for example in 'f' and in 'z', and horizontal curves in the letter 's'. And of course there are a couple of dots, some diagonal lines and plenty of mountainous bumps as well.

Children need to learn and practise these different movements because they need to be able physically to write them, and also get them ingrained in their muscles. They need to learn to see the 'shape' of a word as an aspect of learning to read (it's not all about phonics). At first, children should make these shapes on a large scale, using large movement right from the shoulder. As they get older, and gain more control, the movements become smaller and smaller until they can make the very fine movements needed to hold and control a pencil.

There are a number of key gross and fine motor movements for your children to develop to support their handwriting. These are:

Vertical arcs
Swiping in an up and down movement.

Diagonal arcs
Swiping from side to side, on an angle, in both directions.

Push/Pull/Press:
Large reaching, grasping and pressing movements.

Horizontal arcs
Fanning and wiping from side to side.

Circles
Moving around in a circular, anticlockwise motion.

Note:
The anticlockwise motion is important because of the way letters are written.

These movements simulate the shapes that need to be learned to write letters. For instance, the vertical arc of a lowercase letter 't' or 'l', the sideways snaking motion of a letter 's' and the push to dot a letter 'i'. Get your children to practise these movements on a large scale (with the whole arm), and also gradually on a smaller scale (with the fingers, with a writing tool). The point at which children are ready to make smaller scale shapes will vary a great deal.

Active writing movements

Children love the idea of martial arts movements so get them doing some Kung Fu writing to practise their movements (this idea is inspired by Phil Beadle's *Kung Fu Punctuation* for older writers). Practise the movements and strokes given above, introducing them as Kung Fu style movements for your superhero writers to complete. (In a similar vein, you can 'dance' the strokes alongside stories, songs or rhymes, using the Write Dance materials published by Lucky Duck, 2010.)

To get active with writing, your children could:

- Write giant letter shapes in the air (sky writing).

- Write letter shapes on each other's backs.

- Move ribbons through the air to create the different shapes.

- Paint shapes with 'magic water' (water with glitter in it).

- Draw shapes with a torch in a darkened tent.

- Make shadow shapes with their fingers.

- Write with a 'magic wand', created out of a kitchen roll tube and crepe paper (or a light sabre for any Star Wars fans).

- Trace around shapes and mazes that you have drawn on a sheet of paper.

- Walk around shapes and strokes that you have taped on the floor.

Drawing the strokes in tactile materials works particularly well in encouraging children to feel confident about making different strokes and shapes. It also helps the children to assimilate these strokes fully into their memory. For instance, they might:

- Make large-scale patterns in mud or paint with their fingers or toes.	- Carve shapes in sand using twigs.
- Draw different shapes and strokes in shaving foam, or in whipped cream.	- Make lines and shapes in a piece of clay or play dough.

If you're lucky enough to have access to a beach, there can hardly be any tactile material better than wet sand for practising writing strokes and making shapes with a finger or a stick.

When your children are doing mark making, use vocabulary to describe the kind of movements and shapes that they are making, and encourage them to do the same. For instance, you might talk about how *'I love the way you're sweeping the paint round in circles'*, or *'Those lines you've done are really jagged, aren't they?'*.

The ultimate guide to mark making in the early years

SHAPE WALK

YOU WILL NEED

- An outdoor space or a planned walk somewhere local
- A digital camera
- A clipboard and a pen
- A bag to collect any shapes you find

LEARNING INTENTIONS

- To get the children talking about shapes and using their names
- To explore how shapes can communicate meaning
- To encourage the children to use thinking and questioning skills

INSTRUCTIONS

Take your children on a shape walk – a walk around your local environment during which you collect as many shapes as you can. You might collect a specific item to take back to your setting (a round conker, a spiky leaf) or you could take a photo of a shaped item that cannot be moved (a triangular road sign, a square building). Encourage the children to identify any shapes that have particular meanings for instance a zebra crossing where the different colour symbols indicate that it is safe to cross and zigzag lines indicate that no one should park close by.

When you return to your setting, you could sort the shapes into different types, trace around or over them or make shape collages using a variety of natural materials. All the while, of course, talking about the names of the shapes and the kind of movements needed to make them.

Using stories

Stories have the potential to support your children's pre-writing and writing skills in many different ways. By hearing lots of stories, and looking at plenty of books, children begin to understand the concept that marks on the page hold meaning. In time, they can use those same marks to create meanings and stories of their own.

When young children hear and share stories, they are learning and assimilating vital information about how stories work. They pick up 'story language' words such as 'character', 'hero', 'setting' as well as 'story phrases', 'once upon a time' and 'in a land far far away'. As well as accessing this through books, your children will also be learning it via television and film. The popularity of Disney films, superheroes, cartoon characters, all feeds into your children learning about how stories work and will help them write their own stories as they grow older.

The more explicit you can make this information now, then the better able they will be to use it later on. When you read a story to your children, help them understand the key features of stories. You can do this through discussion, through the way that you tell stories and also through asking questions. Your children need to understand that:

- Stories have a beginning, a middle and an end.

- Stories have a sequence: this event, followed by that event, finishing up with this event.

- Stories use a particular kind of language: openers such as 'Once upon a time' and repeated phrases such as 'Run, run, as fast as you can'.

- Sequences of events are shown through the use of connectives and conjunctions.

- There are different kinds of 'stock' characters within a story: some good (heroes, heroines), some bad (villains, 'baddies').

- Many stories have a happy ending, particularly fairy tales.

Depending on the age of your children, you can introduce different types of story vocabulary. Early on, children might be familiar with words such as 'baddies'; later on this becomes 'villains'. Similarly, words such as 'genre' and 'narrative' can be introduced to school-aged children.

Creating story maps

Story maps are an excellent way to help children understand more about how stories are structured. The basic idea of a story map is that you take a series of events from a story, and map them out visually. This is an activity popularised by author, teacher and writer Pie Corbett in his 'Talk for Writing' approach. The teacher helps the children identify the sequence of events, and these are transformed into a visual representation of the story. While you are creating a story map, you can introduce connectives and conjunctions to the class, words such as: next, then, so and after that. Your visual representation might be:

- On a sheet of A1 size paper, or on a length of lining paper.

- Using pegs to peg up pictures of the events in sequence on a washing line.

- On a storyboard sheet, using photos of each story event as 'stills'.

- Using a set of photocopied pictures, asking the children to work out what order the events appear in the story.

Stories and conceptual development

Of course, stories do a whole lot more for young children than simply show them the link between books and writing; they also introduce a child to layers of meaning far beyond that which they can articulate. The power of stories to support the development of crucial concepts (as outlined in the sections below) means that the frequent and regular use of stories is an essential element in any early years setting.

Developing imagination

Stories require us to use our imaginations – to create a mental picture of something that is not real. When they read a picture book, the images help the child to create a mental picture. But most children are capable of creating this mental picture without having to see the images. Indeed, if you usually tell stories using a book, try retelling some well-known ones simply with words. Listening out for the words, and pulling out information from them, is a vital skill for children to learn.

Entering the fiction

The understanding that some things are real, while others are made up, is a key stage in children's conceptual development. Young children are very willing to 'enter the fiction' of a story, for instance by playing doctors and nurses in your role play area. They experiment with how they might behave in different situations, as well as enjoying the chance to play at being someone else. Young children find it easy to suspend their disbelief (typically, much easier than older children or adults). A young child will happily talk to a toy baby as though it is real – an adult might feel embarrassed to do the same. By entering lots of different fictional worlds, young children start to make sense of themselves and their place within society. They also start to experiment with symbolism – a twig represents a magic wand in a game involving wizards and witches.

A widening vocabulary

We use a wider, more varied vocabulary when we read and write, than we do when we speak. By hearing lots of stories, children are simultaneously exposed to lots of new words. As they learn to read, children will be able to access a word more easily if they can match it up to a word in their spoken vocabulary. Stories also allow children to hear new (or already known) words in different contexts. They start to see that the same word sound (two, too, to) can mean different things in different situations, or might be pronounced differently depending on its meaning (Reading and reading).

Children learn to extract meaning from the context in which a word is heard, and also through the way that the person reading the story says it. Hearing lots of stories helps children understand the importance of context, subtleties and nuance in gathering meaning. At the same time, the children are developing their comprehension skills. Ask questions after you have told a story to check for understanding and to ensure that the story was pitched at the right level.

Story structure and elements

Stories also help children learn about the use of different tenses, connectives and dialogue – all features that they will eventually use in their own writing. They start to see that different stories fall within different genres. There are stories full of action, fairy tales, myths, ghost stories and so on. Each genre has its own particular 'language' of elements.

Stories often invite the reader/listener to engage in word play. They use rhyme, alliteration, tongue twisters, and other linguistic devices to do with the sound of words. Encourage your children to listen out for alliteration and rhyme, to help them tune into language.

Language and layers of meaning

Listening to stories allows even a very young child to see that language has layers of meaning in it. They encounter tricky concepts such as symbolism and metaphor and, even though they might not yet fully understand them, they begin to place the concepts within their understanding of how texts work. For instance:

Symbolism: Many children's stories use colour symbolism. In *Little Red Riding Hood*, the cloak is red – the colour of danger, and of blood. Similarly, the wolf symbolises the dangers that lurk within the forest.

Metaphor: Many fairy stories use a metaphor to show good triumphing over evil. For example, in *Snow White and the Seven Dwarves*, the evil queen is eventually overcome by the prince's love for Snow White. The dwarves represent different human traits, and the mirror on the wall shows the evil queen's vanity.

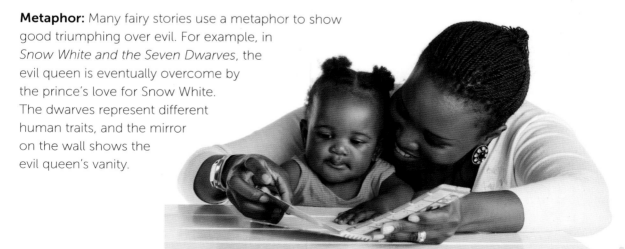

New experiences

Through stories, your children learn about other lives, other experiences, other cultures, other places, other people or other creatures – both real and imagined. Through stories, they can travel to the moon, sail around the world, visit a royal palace or ride on a dragon. Access to new experiences is perhaps particularly important for children who have a limited range of experiences in their lives outside your setting.

Similarly, stories can help your children examine experiences they have gone through, or those that they might face. You can find stories that deal with new or difficult situations such as moving house, a visit to the dentist or the loss of someone close. Through hearing in a story about how someone else has coped with those situations, your children can gain confidence and security.

A sense of place

Stories help us find out about our place in the world, and our place within the history of humanity. Many stories have ancient roots – myths, fables, parables or fairy tales which all go back many hundreds and sometimes even thousands of years. By telling and retelling these stories to each generation, we link ourselves and our children with the storytellers who came before us. Stories can also help us learn about different cultures, or to find out more about our own culture.

Moral codes

Stories often come with a moral code (typically hidden, rather than stated explicitly). They help us understand what is right, and what is wrong. It's no accident that many key religious texts use stories and parables to define a moral code. In an increasingly secular world stories can give us a moral framework by which to live. For instance, in *The Snail and the Whale* (Julia Donaldson and Axel Scheffler, Macmillan, 2004), the moral is that it doesn't matter how big or small you are, what matters is determination and courage. This is what allows the tiny snail to save the whale when it gets beached in the bay. Some children will access the story at its simplest level, as a lovely tale of two creatures with some gorgeous illustrations. But others will pick up the message behind the text, again a key concept for their writing.

Stories also help us learn how different people behave in different situations, and how sometimes they do the right thing, and sometimes they don't. A story can help us see the consequences and outcomes of different kinds of behaviour – both for ourselves, and for others. In this way, they can help your children examine emotions and develop empathy.

Problem solving, sequencing and prediction

Stories offer a great opportunity to get your children thinking about how characters approach and solve problems, and consequently how the children might do the same. How can I build a house that is wolf proof? How can a tiny snail communicate the message that the whale is in danger? How can the mouse in *The Gruffalo* persuade the monster not to eat him? These challenges add dramatic tension to the stories – a crucial element in creating a well-structured piece of fiction.

As they listen to a story, children learn to use prediction: what happens next, what is the cause and effect here, what are the consequences of the characters' actions and decisions? After listening to a story, the children might take that story into their role play, for instance recreating elements of a story or reusing the vocabulary they have heard.

Social interaction

Telling and listening to, a story is of course about social interaction. By sharing stories we build relationships, form bonds and show that we care for each other. And, of course, we should never forget that stories are a huge source of pleasure, both for children and for adults. The act of telling or listening to a story brings people together in a comfortable, relaxed and happy environment.

Helicopter stories

Helicopter stories are a lovely way to support young children's emerging literacy. The practitioner acts as a scribe for the child's ideas, sitting with the child and writing down exactly how s/he tells their story. The class then acts out the story, bringing it back to life off the page. This approach is based on the storytelling work of Vivian Gussin Paley, and you can find out more on the Make Believe Arts website: www.makebelievearts.co.uk.

Enhancing your reading area

By offering a comfortable area for storytelling and story reading, you will help your children associate stories with feeling safe, secure and happy. Their experience at your setting should mirror the experience that they (hopefully) get at home of reading being a warm, cosy and enjoyable activity. Sharing stories at night, safe, snug and warm in their beds with a loved one next to them creates a powerful feeling of security and happiness. Similarly, sharing stories with you and their peer group in your setting can invoke that same feeling. For those children who do not get this kind of opportunity at home, it will be doubly important for you to provide it in your setting.

A lot of the time teachers share stories with a large group or a whole class, with the children relaxing on the carpet as the practitioner reads. Make your carpet area as comfortable as possible – have a selection of cushions or beanbags. Washable or wipe clean cushions can be used for reading stories outdoors in the summer months. During child-initiated times in your setting ensure that children choose to sit and read or look at books. This might be with a practitioner but it might also be something they decide to do with their friends.

To enhance your reading area:

- Try to screen it off, for instance with a partition, by hanging materials from a curtain wire or by using a tent or tepee.

- Offer comfortable seating: a child-sized sofa or a set of beanbags.

- Include a selection of books: both fiction and non-fiction. Depending on the amount of space you have these could be displayed in a book shelf or in a hanging book rack suspended from the wall.

- If space allows, keep your reading area away from any noisy activities.

- Consider using a 'theme' for your reading area. I once saw a beautiful *Winnie the Witch* styled reading area in a Reception class with a blackout tent and torches and bats hanging all around.

Forms of writing

As well as grasping the concept that 'marks hold meaning', your children also need to understand that writing comes in many different forms, and how these forms are used to communicate. In the pre-writing stage these forms of writing might be incorporated into child-initiated play, for instance menus and order pads in a café role play area. In adult-directed activities, the children could create and write in Christmas cards for their parents/carers or write labels to go on a display.

Non-fiction forms

Expose your children to lots of non-fiction forms, both as part of continuous provision and in the displays you have around the place. Put plenty of labels in your teaching space, using large, bold, lower-case print. Here are some of the key non-fiction forms for early years, with tips on how you might use them:

- Labels (the parts of a flower).

- Recipes (to make your mum/dad happy).

- Shopping lists (Santa's list of presents to buy for Christmas).

- Spell ingredients (for a spell to turn you into a princess).

- Postcards (sent home from abroad).

- Birthday cards (for parents or friends).

- Invitations (to the Ugly Sisters in *Cinderella*).

- Posters (about good hand washing).

- Reports (a school report on a character from a book).

- Instructions (how to build a Lego® model).

The image opposite is from a child who had just started in a Reception class. The child had a particular interest in building with Lego® at home and came into school with this set of instructions for building a model. You can see that the child is able to sequence events and write a set of instructions in numbered order, without using words.

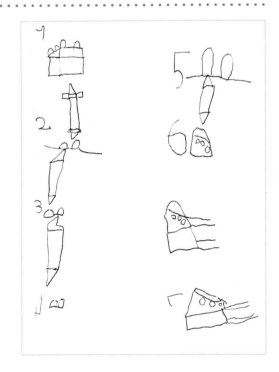

Using frameworks

Writing frames give children a 'frame' on which to hang their ideas. You can use them to introduce the format of different kinds of non-fiction writing, and also to boost children's confidence in creating a similar piece of writing. At the preschool stage, this might be a postcard for them to put in your postbox. In the Reception class and beyond, the frames become more complex, and the children can have more involvement in creating them. Even with young children, you can complete a piece of writing as a whole group, with the children giving the ideas and the practitioner filling in a writing frame.

When using frames:

- Show the children examples of lots of different pieces of writing in this form, e.g. a selection of recipe books.

- Examine the texts closely and talk about the common elements in this form.

- Create a 'frame' for your children on your interactive whiteboard and work together to complete an example.

- Brainstorm a set of key vocabulary with the children, or offer key words on small cards for them to copy.

You can differentiate frames for children of different attainment levels by adapting the amount of 'fill in the blanks' required. You can also give more support to those children who struggle to find the vocabulary they need.

Graphic symbols

Introduce your children to graphic symbols as part of their developing repertoire of mark making. Young children typically understand graphic symbols very early on – the cross on your first aid box, the green arrow pointing to the fire exit. Chinese characters offer a fantastic route into graphic symbols, as in the activity below.

activity ★

HAPPY CHINESE NEW YEAR

YOU WILL NEED

- Large sheets of black paper
- Red paint
- Easels
- A set of the Chinese characters for 'Happy New Year' (an image search on the Internet brings up lots of these)

LEARNING INTENTIONS

- To introduce children to a form of writing from another culture
- To develop understanding about cultures and festivals
- To help the children understand that graphic symbols communicate meaning

INSTRUCTIONS

Introduce the children to the idea of Chinese characters – a set of graphic symbols that stand for words. Show them the characters for 'Happy New Year' and encourage them to paint their own versions of these characters. With older children you might like to talk about how the characters relate to meaning, introducing them to the idea of pictograms (characters that are stylised drawings of what they represent).

Chinese New Year is a great time for doing fine motor/hand to eye coordination activities using chopsticks. Our preschool children love to sing the 'Kung Hei Fat Choy' song each year, and make a Chinese dragon costume so they can dance together for their parents.

Visit the companion website for useful internet links about the Chinese New Year.

Numbers in mark making

Numbers are, of course, a special type of graphic symbol. If you look closely at modern numbers, you can see how the original graphic representations would have turned into the numbers we recognise today. Most of the time we think about writing words when we refer to mark making. However, it is also important for children to learn how to write numbers and use the language of maths.

Numbers often appear in mark making. In the picture opposite, you can see how a child self-initiated a piece of writing involving numbers at the start of Reception class. The child has already picked up that 'ten tens make one hundred' and is using his mark making to convey meaning with numbers.

Writing and meaning making in the home

Those children who see their parents reading at home and whose parents read to them, start to see that reading is both important and pleasurable. Research has shown a clear link between books in the home and positive literacy outcomes for students. A house that is full of books and newspapers, or one where parents regularly visit a library with their children, is a key factor in early literacy. One great way we have found to encourage parents to read with their children at home and to support links between home and preschool, is to publish a weekly blog. Our blog contains information about what the children have been doing that week. It's short and simple but communicates meaning effectively. It also provides a great record of what has been going on in our setting over time. You can read our blog here: www.ourpreschool.org.uk/blog.

One of the best ways to give your children the gift of literacy is to find strategies to encourage parents to read to them regularly. There is a fine balance to be achieved between encouraging parents and lecturing them, so it is wise to tread gently.

Here are some strategies you could try:

- Ask parents to get involved in literacy related tasks, for instance in helping the children to change their book each day.

- Give parents a reading record or reading diary within the child's folder, so that they can record what they've read together.

- Host workshops on reading with your child and generally on how reading is taught in your setting.

- Invite parents in to your setting to share in oral presentations, e.g. poetry reading, storytelling, plays and musicals.

Part 5

I grasp the link between speaking and writing

In this section

- Find out why hearing sounds is crucial for reading and writing

- Help your children build their phonological awareness

- Explore ways of using stories, songs and rhymes

- Get creative with storytelling sessions

Consider this...

The process of learning to read and write is a bit like taking apart, and then reassembling, a piece of flat pack furniture. In order to read, the child must be able to break down the words into their constituent parts, i.e. the letter sounds, blends and syllables. This is referred to as 'decoding' language. Then, in order to write, the child must fit those sounds together to build the words back up again. This is often referred to as 'encoding' language. In order to pick apart and reassemble the words, a child must be able to hear and discriminate the sounds *within* words. Learning how to do this is a vital step in getting ready to read and write.

We live in an increasingly noise filled society. Many of the noises that our children hear are man-made, rather than natural, ones. A backdrop of constant radio, television, computer games or music can make it hard for children to distinguish individual sounds. Even outdoors, children who live in the city will be exposed to the constant background buzz of cars, lorries and aeroplanes. It can be incredibly hard for them to focus in on talk, language and sounds, so you need to offer them lots of chances to do just that. A recent report from the World Health Organization confirmed that excessive noise can impact on children's language development and cognitive functioning. See the companion website for links. (website)

A word of warning

The current push in England towards the teaching of reading solely via systematic synthetic phonics (SSP), and the accompanying phonics test in Year 1, might tempt you to believe that learning to read is *only* about sound. However, it's important to understand that English is not a regular language. There are many words which break the rules, and that are impossible to spell via phonics-based methods alone. Just think for a moment of bough, cough, enough, though and through. It's also perfectly possible to learn to read using other methods. The current focus on SSP is to do with efficiency for the majority of children, rather than it being the only possible method. (I am living proof of this, since I learned to read in the days of whole word sight methods.)

A child who relies solely on phonic knowledge to read and write may end up misspelling words. Just like letters, words create a shape, as well as being a collection of sounds. Words such as 'the' and 'once' (sometimes referred to as 'tricky' or 'red' words) do not comply to regular patterns of sound, so are tricky to decode using phonics, but they are simple to learn by sight.

Studying sounds

To develop phonological awareness, offer your children lots of opportunities to study sounds, and to listen closely. Auditory discrimination is hugely important in the development of both reading and writing. Being able to pick out and identify the sounds within words allows children to unlock the code of written and spoken language. They also start to hear how words can have similar sounds within them, or at the end, as with rhyming words. In order to be able to distinguish letter sounds, one from another, there are three important things that children need to be able to do:

1. **Detection**: I can hear when the sound happens.

2. **Discrimination**: I can hear when the sound changes.

3. **Identification**: I can hear what the sound actually is.

So long as you are sure that your children do not have physical problems with hearing, your focus as a practitioner will be on helping the child develop the second and third aspects of auditory processing. By doing lots of activities based around hearing, studying and identifying sounds, your children will be best placed to pick out letter sounds and turn those sounds into the written word. There are lots of ideas opposite to give you inspiration.

The ultimate guide to mark making in the early years

SOUND ACTIVITIES (INSTRUMENTS)

- Listen to the sounds of different instruments and objects. Hide the instrument or object, for instance behind a sheet, and ask the children what they can hear.

- Get the children to make shakers out of plastic bottles with different objects inside. Try rice, beads, pasta, coins, etc. What different sounds do they make?

- Ask your children to experiment with making loud sounds and quiet sounds, using instruments. They might do this as a whole group, or individually. Which instruments are good for making really loud sounds? Which instruments tend to make sounds that are very quiet?

SOUND ACTIVITIES (OBJECTS AND RESOURCES)

- Take a moneybox and drop coins into it, one at a time. Can the children tell how many coins are in the box?

- Hide an item in a box and shake it. Ask the children to guess what the object is from the noise that it makes.

- Show the class a puppet (animals, dinosaurs). What sound would it make? Can they create a sound effect for the puppet?

SOUND EFFECTS AND SOUND TRACKING

- Talk about the sounds that animals make. Identify different animals by listening to the sounds they make online or on a CD.

- Use a listening centre with headphones to play soundtracks in a 'listening area'. Ask the children to identify the different sounds they hear on the soundtrack.

- Visit the website www.freesound.org for some interesting and unusual sounds. This is a creative commons database where people share sound effects that you can use with your children for free.

TALKING AND THINKING ABOUT SOUNDS

- Go on a listening walk and collect examples of sounds as you walk.

- Extend this by collecting samples of sounds, using a recording device. When you get back to your setting, play the sounds back and try to remember what it was you heard.

- Get your children to talk about what sounds they like, what sounds they don't like, and why.

MAKING SOUNDS WITH YOUR BODIES

- Stamp, splash and stomp through mud or water, echoing the sounds you make with your voices as you do it.

- Swish through leaves with your feet on an autumn walk.

- Clap, jump, wave and make accompanying sounds.

- Tap your hands on your knees together, on the floor, and on your tummies.

If you're in a setting where you have children with EAL, invite parents who speak other community languages to come in and talk to the children. Talk with the children about how the letter sounds are pronounced differently in other languages.

SOUNDS AND NATURE

- Use a wide range of natural materials to create sounds. Which natural materials make the best or most interesting sounds?

- Go for a 'sounds walk' and see how many animal sounds and sounds from nature you can hear and note down.

- Invite people to bring animals into your setting. This is especially easy in a rural setting like ours. We've had chicks, sheep, goats, alpacas, owls and many more to visit! In an urban area, get in touch with your local city farm if you have one close by.

- Encourage the children to find lots of animal sound effects for a single animal, e.g. a dog goes woof, wuff, bark, yap and yip.

The ultimate guide to mark making in the early years

Developing your listening area

Have a listening area on offer as part of your continuous provision. Here are some dos and don'ts for making the most of this area:

Do

- Situate your listening area away from noisy activities.

- If possible, find some way to screen it off from distractions.

- Have headphones, so children can listen individually.

- Have signs/symbols for 'quiet' on display: a finger to a lip, a hand to an ear.

Don't

- Have too many busy, distracting displays around your listening area.

- Let too many children use it at any one time.

- Put the instruments out for the children to use on the same day as your listening centre.

Auditory processing difficulties (APD)

When you're doing activities around sounds, and discriminating letter sounds within words, you may find that some of your children seem to struggle. Although a difficulty in hearing sounds might indicate a physical problem with hearing (see p. 52) for how to identify this) it may also indicate a problem with the processing of auditory information. What this means is that the problem is in the brain, rather than in the signal coming from the ears.

If you notice that a child frequently displays any of the following behaviours, it may be that they have problems processing auditory information. If you are unsure, you should always refer the child for a specialist evaluation. Concerns should be raised if the child:

- Appears to have problems understanding instructions.

- Speaks very little, or finds it hard to work out what s/he wants to say.

- Tends to lose focus, particularly when you are speaking to the group.

- Struggles to hear and focus when there is lots of background noise.

Interestingly, children who are diagnosed as having ADHD often display very similar symptoms to those listed above. The following strategies will support and help a child with APD, and indeed are good practice any time you address the class

- When you say something to the group, give them something to look at as well: a picture, a toy, a visual back up.

- Use the sound of your voice to give cues to the child – emphasise key words, vary the pace.

- When you're giving instructions, do not use excess words. Keep it short and to the point.

- Emphasise key words by putting stress on them.

- Use hand gestures to help the children understand what you are saying.

- Support the children as they start an activity, to ensure they have understood what you said.

- If any children you teach have hearing problems get them to sit near the front when you are addressing the whole group.

- When you're introducing important concepts, ideas or new skills, use lots of repetition and real life examples.

Songs, rhymes and poems

As every early years educator knows, songs, rhymes and poems are a wonderful way to get children tuning in to language. These forms are perfect for developing young children's language because they:

- Help children learn vocabulary through lots of repetition.

- Help children listen out for similar sounds within language, e.g. the rhymes within pat, cat, bat and mat.

- Have key phrases which are repeated, that the child can quickly learn.

- Allow the children to join in with each other, and build confidence about speaking and singing.

- Use simple beats and tunes, which are catchy and easy to remember.

- Often have matching movements or gestures, which back up the children's comprehension, make them easier to remember and encourage fine and gross motor movements.

- Often use alliteration, and are therefore good for picking out letter sounds ('Wee Willie Winky').

- Often use gradually decreasing numbers (e.g. '10 Green Bottles'), which are also great for counting activities.

- Have movements which improve motor skills (the 'pull, pull, clap, clap, clap' of 'Wind the Bobbin Up').

- Are often known and loved by parents too, so offer a great way to link the home with the setting.

- Are a key part of oral heritage, passed on from generation to generation.

There are hundreds of nursery rhymes you can use with your children. You can find a list of some favourites on my website. Visit www.suecowley.co.uk/100-nursery-rhymes.html. Some of the favourites in our setting are:

- 'Wind the Bobbin Up'
- 'The Wheels on the Bus'
- 'Twinkle Twinkle Little Star'
- 'Head, Shoulders, Knees and Toes'

- 'Dingle Dangle Scarecrow'
- 'Humpty Dumpty'
- 'Incey Wincey Spider'

Create time to sing nursery rhymes throughout your sessions or your day. You could sing them at snack time, as you move around the setting, in a whole class group, in small groups, outdoors, on a walk around the local area, in the morning and at going home time. If it's raining, grab your coats, wellies and umbrellas to go outside and sing Rain, rain, go away! When using songs and rhymes with your children, encourage them to:

- Clap along with the rhythm, or tap it out on a drum.

- Join in with the words – first a single repeated phrase, gradually building up until they know the whole rhyme.

- Copy the actions as you do them then repeat these each time you sing the song.

- Keep in time with a regular beat as you clap it or beat it out.

- Nominate favourites, for you to sing.

- Tell you what letter sounds they can spot.

You can also play around with songs, for instance by getting the children to:

- Sing faster, then sing slower (present this as 'singing in slow motion', then in 'super fast time').

- Sing louder, then sing quieter.

- Sing higher, then lower (accompany this by standing on tiptoes, then crouching down low).

You can also use props to spice up song time for your children. Have a box where you store resources so that you can use them whenever you have a spare moment. In our nursery rhymes box we have the props to accompany lots of different songs, including 'Five Fat Sausages' (i.e. a saucepan and some sausages).

The ultimate guide to mark making in the early years

Rhymes

Rhymes and rhyming poems make use of phonemes, and are a great way to show children how learning one sound ('ay') can lead to learning how to write and spell many other words ('say', 'day', 'stay' and so on). When you're using poems or rhyming stories with your children:

- Encourage them to join in with the rhyming or repeated parts: 'Run, run, as fast as you can, you can't catch me, I'm the gingerbread man'.

- Do the actions together, along with the story: 'So he huffed and he puffed... and he huffed and he puffed'.

- Link rhymes to events, e.g. 'I can sing a rainbow' when you see one, or 'Frosty the snowman' in the winter time.

- Have objects that link to the rhymes to provide a visual support for the children, e.g. a toy cat, a hat, a mat, a toy rat and a bat.

Alliteration

Alliteration is a great way to get the children picking out the letter sounds within speech. After a while as an early years educator, you will probably find yourself alliterating without even thinking about it: 'Lucy, that's a lovely lunchbox, you lucky little thing'. Tongue twisters, such as 'She sells sea shells on the sea shore' are a great way into alliteration (and also into encouraging children to think about how they use their mouth and speech muscles to make letter sounds).

To inspire the use of alliteration in your setting...

- Fill a set of boxes or bags with objects that start with the same sound, for when you are sharing letter sounds with the children. (Similar themed boxes can be used to inspire stories for older children. For instance, a box full of pirate related objects and another box with toy dinosaurs, fossils and jungle plants.)

- Find opportunities to use alliterative phrases in everyday situations. Simply adding an alliterative word to the children's names is a good start. So, you might have a 'Magic Martha', an 'Amazing Ahmed' and a 'Chipper Charlie'.

- Hide alliterative objects in the sand tray and ask the children what the starting letter of the objects is.

- Show the children what your mouth does when you make a 't' sound or a 'p', and get them to make the same muscular movements.

- Use mirrors so that children can see what their mouths do when they make different sounds.

The joy of stories

One of the true joys of working in early years and primary is the chance to share stories daily with your children. There is something magical about a group of children mesmerised by a story being read to them. The children feel relaxed and secure when they are being read a story. Often little children will lie down, flop backwards, or even doze off.

One day our children will progress to writing stories of their own, so we need to show them how magical the story world can be. One of the key skills of the early years practitioner is to be able to tell a story in a way that engrosses and captivates the children. The best storytellers bring the story to life, by using every skill at their disposal. At first, it can feel a bit silly going over the top with the voice that you use, or making the faces of different characters. But the more lively and multisensory your telling of the story is, the more entranced your children will be. To get the very best out of stories in your setting:

- Give the children time to fall completely silent before you tell a story. Use a pause and non-verbal interventions to encourage them to give you their attention.

- Use big books whenever you can, so that all the children can see the words and pictures.

- Hold the book facing the group, and to one side of you, so that you can read it easily and the children can see it the right way up.

- Alternatively, hold the book in front of you, and learn the skill of reading upside down!

- Make the most of tone. It is impossible to overdo the use of tone with this age group. Sound really excited, really scared or really angry.

- Modulate the speed of your voice, to show where excitement is building up, and when there is a calmer section. Use a fast, breathless pace to show urgency or fear, and a slow, soft pace for quieter, calmer bits of the story.

- Play around with volume levels as well. If you spot that the children are losing focus, try leaning forwards slightly and speaking really quietly, to encourage them to listen closely.

- Use facial expressions, both to help you communicate meaning and emotion to the children, but also because this will help you add tone to your voice.

Consider using a large puppet to help you tell the story, or play one of the characters in the story yourself. This can help you feel a bit less silly about doing funny voices and using lots of tone. It is also very captivating for the children, who are quite happy to go along with the 'fiction' of a puppet helping you tell a story.

Interactive stories

Modern children are brought up in a highly interactive world, one that is fundamentally different to that of only 20 or 30 years ago. Digital television, the Internet, electronics, computer games and computerised toys – all now offer a two way flow of information and ideas to children. For instance, the story books that read to you when you press a button, or the toy that asks you to respond to an instruction 'bop it!'; similarly, the red dot that pops up on the TV screen, or the touch screen technology of a handheld console or a mobile phone. Our children are used to interactivity, and there is little point in us complaining how children used to concentrate better or how they managed on a single hour of children's TV a day.

Accept the interactive nature of the modern world by finding ways to make your storytelling sessions an interactive, multisensory experience. You will find that this is particularly important if you work with very young children, or children who struggle with concentration levels. Develop the ability to 'read' the group so that you quickly realise when they are beginning to lose their focus and you need to make the story more engaging. Look out for signs such as children fidgeting, looking away and starting to bother each other. Learn to read the story with one eye, while simultaneously reading the group's levels of focus with the other.

To make a story interactive as you tell it, you can:

- Get the children to become characters in the story, for instance standing up to 'climb' trees and 'swing' through the vines in a story about the jungle.

- Add props to engage the children's interest, for example straw, twigs and bricks for the children to see, handle or blow over while you are telling the story of *The Three Little Pigs*.

- Add 'invisible' props to encourage an imaginative response, for instance you asking the children to hold and stroke a frightened cat, while telling them the story of *The Lighthouse Keeper's Lunch* (Ronda and David Armitage, Scholastic, 2007).

- Add costumes, such as hats and gloves, for instance asking volunteers to wear the clothes from the story of *The Smartest Giant in Town* (Julia Donald and Axel Scheffler, Macmillan, 2003).

- Encourage the children to add sound effects, e.g. all joining in as the Giant says 'Fee Fi Fo Fum', or making the sound of the Billy Goats Gruff trip trapping across the bridge.

- Do some team storytelling where one person tells the story, while the second person makes the voices, points at the pictures or does the actions.

Bring stories to life after the event as well, for example after reading the story of *The Lighthouse Keeper's Lunch*, you might make the lunch and then invent a basket and pulley system to get it across to the lighthouse. Challenge the children to think of ways to keep those pesky seagulls at bay!

Part 6

I feel confident about communicating

In this section

- Help your children build confidence in communicating

- Encourage your children to express opinions

- Incorporate drama activities to boost self esteem

- Use the 'Role of the Expert' to improve confidence

- Consider how to use marking in the most constructive way

Consider this...

Communication, by its nature, involves more than one person. This book can only communicate ideas and information because of its relationship to you, the person reading it. You act as an audience for what is on the pages, bringing it to life and giving it meaning. If it sat on a shelf, gathering dust, it would communicate nothing to anybody, even though the words were there inside its pages. When we communicate, whether through speech or writing, the way that an audience responds and reacts is fundamental to the experience.

In many ways, writing is a risky business, requiring a great deal of confidence from the writer. When you create a piece of writing, you put your own thoughts, ideas and opinions down on paper. But what if the audience doesn't like what you have written, or how you have written it? As educators, we often sit in judgement on our children's writing, to see whether it matches up to expected standards. The way that we respond and react can either boost or damage self-confidence and motivation to write in the future.

When we write, an internal editor sits on our shoulders – the inner voice that tells us 'you can't say that' or 'that sounds silly'. But listening to this voice can stifle a writer's confidence, so take care that you don't become the equivalent of an internal editor for the children you teach. Our ultimate aim is for our children to become confident communicators, inspired to express themselves and share their ideas. Writing is not about simply meeting targets – it is an act of communication.

Building confident communicators

Each child you work with is a unique individual. Some children are confident and outgoing, others are cripplingly shy. Some prefer to sit back and let others take the lead, others are the leader in every peer group situation. A confident attitude is influenced by many factors. Where children have secure early attachments (caring parents, a strong family network) this can help boost confidence. It's worth thinking about what we mean by confidence. A confident person:

- Is self-assertive.

- Has high self-esteem.

- Feels that their ideas matter.

- Is happy to express their opinions and speak out.

- Is resilient when things go wrong and can 'bounce back' from setbacks.

- Knows how to handle criticism and how to put critique to good use.

You can support your children and build their confidence in many ways. However, you can also damage young children's confidence unintentionally. If you think back to when you were at school you may have had teachers who damaged your self-confidence, perhaps without realising they were doing it. The following lists of dos and don'ts will help you think about how you can support your children in building self-confidence:

Do

- Listen with interest to what they have to say (and even if you're not particularly interested at that precise moment, at least look like you are).

- Encourage them to develop what they say through open-ended questioning techniques.

- Join in with their play and show that you enjoy the time you spend with them.

- Take their emotions seriously, never brushing them aside.

- Set targets or activities that stretch them, but which they can access and be successful at.

- Respect their interests and find activities that fit with these.

- Acknowledge that sometimes you find things difficult, just like they do.

- Let them know that it is okay to take risks, to make mistakes and to get things wrong.

- Let them try new things, even if they are not yet good at them.

- Encourage them to be independent learners, and independent in self-care.

- Remember that dismissive comments and difficult situations affect us much more deeply when we are young.

Don't

- Laugh at them if they do something wrong.

- Use dismissive language – words such as 'silly'.

- Tell them what to do all the time, using lists of demands.

- Even if they are being particularly difficult, or you're having a bad day, don't let your emotions come through in your tone of voice or expressions.

- Use lots of closed questions, which don't allow them to express their ideas.

- Set targets that they will struggle to reach.

- Nitpick or nag, even if you are feeling stressed.

- Complain when they make a mess, if it is a valid part of their learning.

- Brush off their concerns. Make sure you acknowledge when they are worried or nervous about something (even if you feel it is silly).

It is important to be aware that you may like some children you work with more than others but you need to make a conscious effort not to have favourites. Ask yourself (and be honest):

> Do I pick some children more often than others to answer questions during whole class/group time?

> If I'm honest, are there some children I prefer and does this perhaps come out in the way that I treat them?

> Do I ever allow negative feelings about the children to come out in the way that I talk to and interact with them?

> Am I ever dismissive of some children's ideas, or do I see less value in what some children say than others?

The secret when working with children is to acknowledge your personal feelings but to take a professional approach. In other words, try your very hardest not to let your feelings affect your behaviour towards them.

Using praise and target setting

We all like to be told that we have done something well but, to be of value, praise needs to be genuine and focused. We can all benefit from having targets to work towards but again these need to be realistic for us to achieve. You won't create self-confident children by telling them that everything they do is great (no matter whether it is or not). Research has shown that it is far more effective to praise a child for the effort put into things than for the level of achievement attained.

Being able to praise a child for effort relies on your knowledge of individual children. Some may be able to achieve a great piece of writing without much effort at all. For others, a single sentence could represent a huge milestone. Your use of targets depends a great deal on the child as well. Some will benefit from a hefty push; others will crumble unless you are very careful in how you phrase constructive criticism.

Making the most of praise

When you praise a piece that a child has done, avoid vague generalisations about how 'good' or not it is. Try not to comment on the child's individual aptitude or use words like clever or intelligent, e.g.

> *'Wow, what a great picture, aren't you clever!'*

The best praise gives specific, detailed comments which highlight exactly what it is about the child's work that is good:

> *'I really like the way that you've used red paint to show how the volcano is overflowing.'*

Similarly, when you're praising a child's mark making or writing, avoid generalised comments such as:

> *'That's such a great poem, aren't you a clever girl?'*

Instead, talk specifically about what the child has done well:

> *'I love the way you've used alliteration in your poem to echo the sounds of the fireworks.'*

Setting targets

Alongside the use of praise to boost confidence, give targets for future improvement. A useful ratio is one target for improvement, for every three positive comments ('Three Stars and a Wish' approach as explained on p. 102). Make sure the targets you set:

- Are clear and specific.

- Involve improving one aspect, rather than lots.

- Are realistic and achievable.

- Are supportive and kindly phrased.

- Encourage the children to push themselves that bit further.

Practising using praise and targets

A good way to improve your use of praise and targets is to practise using them. Below you will see a piece of child-initiated writing, done by a five-year-old who is already a fluent reader. Consider how you might respond to this piece of writing:

- What would you say to the child about the positive aspects of what they have written?

- What could the child do next time to improve the writing further?

- Clearly, there are a number of technical issues with this piece of writing. Which one would you pick for the child to work on and improve?

- What are the next steps for this child to move on in terms of writing?

- Would you write your comments on the piece, or would it work better to give verbal feedback?

Marking writing

As children begin to write more fluently, you will begin to give evaluative comments on their writing to help them improve. The key to ensuring that this process is confidence-building, rather than destroying, is to strike a balance between targeted praise and constructive criticism. This will vary according to the needs of the child.

Most teachers will have worked with children whose writing is incredibly weak and strewn with errors. Intuitively, we know that to highlight every error within a hard-won piece of writing could devastate the child. Marking needs to be a constructive dialogue between teacher and child, one that is supportive but that still pushes the child to do a bit better next time around.

In the old days, marking involved putting a big red tick or cross at the end of a child's work and perhaps a brief comment. However, it is now understood that this kind of marking is pretty much pointless. Instead, we try to ensure that our assessment is for learning, that it informs and supports learning as well as assessing it. For marking to be effective in helping a child improve their writing, it needs to:

- Give details about what works well.

- Set a clear target for future improvement.

- Be understood by the child.

- Explain to the child how to improve on this aspect (for instance writing a misspelt word in the back of the book).

- Be read and responded to by the child. Set aside time for this when handing back writing (this is sometimes referred to 'DIRT'— 'dedicated improvement and reflection time).

Visual marking

You can use a highlighter pen to identify the aspects of writing that work well and areas you want the child to target next. Use the same colours every time you mark. The usual choice is pink for the good bits and green for the bits the child could improve. Make sure that your children (and their parents) understand why you are using these colours and what they mean. Ensure too that you take account of any children who might have a colour vision deficiency (what we used to call colour blindness).

Three stars and a wish

This technique allows you to identify what has worked well in a piece and give a target for future improvement. The 'three stars' are three aspects of the writing that work well; the 'wish' is the area that you'd like the child to work on further. Your children can also use this approach when doing peer assessment.

My opinion matters

Part of being self-confident is feeling as though your ideas and opinions matter and that you are going to be taken seriously. Find ways to let your children express their opinions, and influence the choices that are made within your setting or school. For instance they could:

- Choose what they want to play with, using a 'choices board'.

- Tell you about their favourite resources, and about any new ones they would like to have.

- Put forward their ideas at circle time or as part of a school council.

- Have an influence on the way that you structure your day, for instance deciding when you tell a whole class story.

- Take a vote on the next storybook that you read to them.

- Share their thoughts about what matters to them, for instance showing a favourite toy at 'Show and Tell'.

- Share their news with you on a Monday morning.

- Choose a topic for writing or identify questions they want answered in class.

Open-ended discussion

One of the key ways to support your children in feeling that their ideas have value is through the use of open-ended discussion techniques. This is a key skill for early years educators but it can be surprisingly difficult to do. Often, we fall into a verbal style that involves lots of instructions and directions ('tidy up', 'put on your coats'). We also tend to use lots of closed questions ('who has finished their work?') and indeed rhetorical questions too ('why are you being so noisy?'). This may be because of an urge to 'get through' the learning, to keep the children 'under control' or simply because it becomes a matter of habit over time.

In early years settings, open-ended discussions are often referred to as sustained shared thinking, i.e. a conversation between the adult and child in which they work together to support and extend thinking. When considering how we use speech, it is helpful to think about the different kinds of talk we use.

Instructions/directions: The practitioner tells the child what to do. The child is expected to comply, rather than questioning what has been said. Sometimes these are phrased as a rhetorical question ('can you build me a tower?').

For example:

> *'I want you to build me a tower with ten blocks.'*
>
> *'Find the circle in this picture.'*
>
> *'We've finished building our Little Pigs' house, now we're all going to tidy up the straw.'*

Closed questions: The practitioner asks questions that only have one correct answer, usually requiring a short one or two word response. The child's answer is either right or wrong. Closed questions have their place as a test of knowledge or understanding. However, they tend to shut down any chance of a conversation or of higher order thinking, e.g.

'How many blocks are in your tower?'

'Can you find three different shapes in this picture?'

'What is the first house in the story of The Three Little Pigs made of?'

Open questions: These are questions that open up a discussion, and which do not have a single 'correct' answer. They are often to do with feelings, opinions or ideas. There is no right or wrong answer: whatever the child says can be valid and valued, e.g.

'What's that you're making? It looks interesting, could you tell me about it?'

'Who can tell me what their favourite thing is about this picture?'

'I was thinking we could make some houses, like in the Three Little Pigs story that we read earlier. Has anyone got any ideas about what they would like to make their house from?'

Open-ended questioning is valuable because:

- It encourages the use of lateral thinking and higher order thinking skills such as theorising and deduction.

- It can help you find ways to solve a problem, together with the children.

- It allows you to help the children understand concepts.

- It builds the children's confidence in feeling that their ideas and opinions matter.

- It helps us consider the 'big questions' of life – it is a philosophical technique.

- It allows the adult to build on what the children already know, moving the discussion in the most appropriate direction.

The ultimate guide to mark making in the early years

Sustained shared thinking

When you observe children's play and judge that it would be useful for you to become involved, you can use open-ended questioning to move the thinking and ideas forwards and to develop the children's talk. This kind of discussion is useful for helping children understand how to develop ideas, elaborate thinking and consider perspectives – all skills that will prove crucial in their writing. During this process you might use some or all of the following techniques:

TUNE IN

- Listen carefully to what the child is saying.

- 'Read' the body language.

- Watch the play before you intervene.

TAKE AN INTEREST

- Give the child your full attention.

- Make eye contact and smile.

- Ask open questions about their play.

ENCOURAGE THEM TO ELABORATE OR SUMMARISE

Say:

- 'I'd really love to hear more about that.'

- 'That's very interesting, could you show me again?'

- 'So you made that bit first did you?'

- Share your experiences and ideas.

- Tell a story about when you did something similar.

- Offer a suggestion as to how the child might do something.

- Use focused praise and targets.

- Highlight what the child has done well.

- Suggest something they might try next.

- Offer fresh perspectives.

- Identify an alternative viewpoint on the issue.

- Encourage the child to think about what others might do/feel/say/think.

- Model your thought processes.

- Use vocabulary around thinking when you talk with the child.

- Explain your own thinking processes.

This last step is known as metacognition (the process of thinking about what we are thinking), becoming aware of our own thought processes.

Group activities and circle time

Group activities are one of the best scenarios for boosting confidence and self-esteem, so long as they are well managed. In a group, we can share and develop ideas, work together to achieve things, solve problems, boost relationships and so on. It is not hard to see why circle time is so popular with children of this age. The format of a circle is very inclusive. Everyone can see each other, and we can easily share thoughts and ideas.

When using a circle:

- Get the children to stand in a proper circular shaped circle. Encourage them to think about the structure of a circle and what it means to them.

- Allow children to 'pass' if they don't want to contribute. Never put them on the spot or force a quiet child to take part.

- Use circles of different sizes – sometimes a whole class or group but other times a smaller circle so that shy children are more likely to contribute.

- Praise the children for good 'circle time behaviours' such as listening carefully, taking turns and so on.

Here are some suggestions for simple circle time activities:

- Talking Ted: each child holds the teddy and tells the group one thing.

- Pass the animal: as they pass it around, they say one thing about the animal, e.g. for a toy cow 'a cow is black and white', 'a cow gives us milk'.

- My news: one thing they did over the weekend.

- Free association: give the children a theme, for instance 'water' and ask them to say a word that links to the theme, e.g. cold, hot, pool, tap, hose.

- Pass a tambourine around, as each child gets it, they tap out the syllables of their name.

- Ask the children to each tell you their favourite thing, based on a theme. For instance, my favourite TV programme, my favourite food, or my favourite toy.

- Sing a song and do the actions together.

- Play 'leader of the band': one volunteer shuts their eyes, while you choose a leader. That child leads the band in a series of movements – tapping hands on knees, clapping hands, tapping shoulders, etc. The volunteer must try to figure out who the 'leader of the band' is; the rest of the children must try to change movements at the same moment as the leader, to stop their identity from being revealed.

- Pass a toy animal around the circle, for instance a toy guinea pig, but ask the children to act as though it is real. Encourage the children to handle it gently, comfort it and so on. You can also do this with an invisible pet.

- And of course, all the old favourites, such as 'Chinese Whispers', 'Wink Murder', 'Fruit Salad', 'Simon Says', and so on.

The 'role of the expert'

Role of the expert is a fantastic drama technique for boosting children's confidence and encouraging them to take an independent and mature approach to learning. It is sometimes referred to as 'mantle of the expert'. This technique is most useful within role play and drama activities and it works well for doing in-role writing. With older children you can use it as a way into other subject areas, for instance science (forensic experts, scientists at a government laboratory). The idea of the technique is that:

- The children assume the role of an expert of some kind: a doctor, a vet, a police officer, a superhero.

- They use this role within the drama, for instance working as a doctor in a hospital-based role play.

- They take on the attributes and attitudes of the character they are playing.

- They use the kind of language and vocabulary that this expert would use in real life.

- The teacher can guide the direction of the drama, from inside the fiction.

The benefits of 'role of the expert' include:

- The children tend to take on more mature attitudes and responses while working within a role.

- The practitioner can ask them to do mark making or writing activities that this 'expert' would do (for instance making notes about a patient).

- The role they have taken on can boost their confidence through the idea of becoming someone else who is an 'expert' on a subject or area.

- The teacher can help control the role play from inside the drama by taking on a role within the scenario.

Part 7

I am inspired to make marks

In this section

- Give your children a real reason for writing

- Inspire your children with imaginative approaches

- Boost motivation to write for all children

- Use provocations and challenges to make writing engaging

- Find ideas for themes to inspire mark making

Consider this...

As we move ever further into the digital age, writing with a pencil and paper as opposed to typing on a keyboard becomes ever less common. Even though I am a professional writer, it is fairly rare for me to put pen to paper as opposed to fingers to keyboard. Similarly, 'snail mail' seems rather slow and old fashioned compared to email and text messaging. What this means is that children are less likely to see parents or carers putting pen to paper at home. In turn, it is ever more important for them to see practitioners and teachers doing this in an early years setting.

Throughout their years of education, it is crucial for children to have a good reason to write. We must encourage them to feel an urge to write, rather than seeing it as a chore, if our hope is for them to become skilled and avid writers. Writing is hard work, especially for those children who have any kind of literacy related SEND. Too often we tell our pupils that they have to write to meet targets or to pass exams. But this is not a genuine reason to write. A piece of writing only comes to life when it has a real audience (an interested reader) to interact with it. If we want our children to achieve their best writing, they must feel motivated to communicate.

Inspirational mark making

There are certain key features that tend to inspire children (and people of any age) to engage with an activity. When you're looking to create inspirational mark making activities, make sure that the activity, or the resources that accompany it, fulfil some or all of the following criteria:

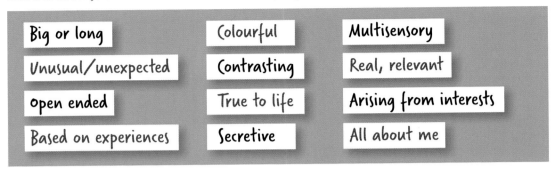

Here are some ideas about how to utilise these approaches with your children:

Big/long: Make the writing area unusually big or long so that it offers the children a giant, supersized canvas, e.g. you could wrap a climbing frame completely in lining paper, so that the children can create the outline of a castle on it.

Unusual: Get the children writing on an unusual backdrop: a wall, a large sheet of cardboard, a bed sheet or the ground. Set up the activity in an unusual place: under a desk, on the ceiling, as a treasure hunt around the grounds.

Colourful/contrasting: Black and white or black and silver – both work well for writing about space. Red and black make a great graphic contrast symbolising fire or danger.

Multisensory: Put sandpaper letter shapes in a bag to see if the children can identify them by touch alone. Get your children splashing in the water or playing in the snow, and then writing about how it felt.

Arising from interests: A focus on superheroes, with a superhero den on offer for children who show a fascination with these characters, or a focus on writing cartoons for children who love comics.

Based on experience: A trip to a museum, to a movie that they have seen recently or a diary kept while on holiday. The immediacy and vibrancy of the experience makes the writing feel real and purposeful.

Secretive: Children love the idea of things being hidden, or having to be kept secret. An envelope on the desks, saying 'Do not Open' will provoke all sorts of interest and engagement.

All about me: We all love to talk about ourselves and writing is the epitome of something that is 'all about me'. Even if we are not doing an autobiographical piece, our writing is still an expression of who we are and what we think and feel.

Here are some examples of writing inspired by some of the opposite feature.

Arising from interests/based on experiences

In this piece of self-initiated writing, the Reception aged child had been to see the Disney Pixar film WALL·E. The child was inspired to draw the characters from the film and write about how WALL·E 'saff his pinit' ('saves his planet'). Notice how the parts of the characters are labelled, including arms and 'bonit' (bonnet).

Multisensory/based on experiences (All about me)

This piece of writing was done in a holiday diary at the end of Year 1. The teacher had asked the children to keep a diary of what they did during their holidays. You can sense the thrill the child felt and the urgency of trying to get across how it felt to go to the water park.

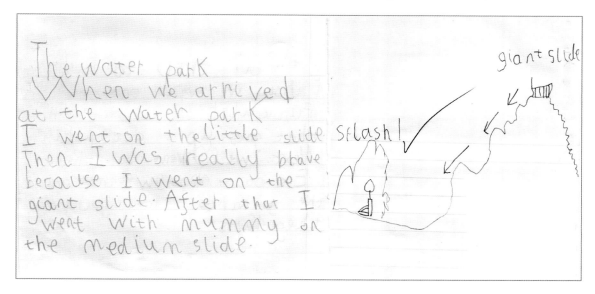

Creating a writing area

Show that writing really matters within your setting by having an area dedicated solely to writing. Think carefully about how you set this out and the kind of resources you have on offer. It is a good idea to have a unit in which to store various resources. It is fun to make your writing area look a bit like an office. By keeping the area tidy, and the resources in tip-top condition, you show that you view writing as important and worthwhile.

Writing area checklist

You can find a downloadable copy of this checklist on the companion website. *website*

Resource	Tick
Postcards	❏
Pencils, pens, felt tips, biros, markers	❏
Letter writing paper	❏
Envelopes in all different sizes	❏
Pads and notebooks	❏
Paper in a variety of types, sizes, colours and textures	❏
Clipboards (A4 and also small size)	❏
Scissors	❏
Sticky notes	❏
Sticky labels	❏
Comics and magazines	❏
A postbox	❏
A word bank	❏
A set of magnetic letters/words	❏

Resource	Tick
Alphabet stencils	❏
Bulldog clips, paper clips	❏
Stapler	❏
Hole punch	❏
Treasury tags	❏
Rulers	❏
Glue sticks	❏
Sticky tape in a dispenser	❏
Masking tape	❏
Pre-printed forms	❏
Child's dictionary	❏
Folders	❏
Telephone	❏
Mini whiteboards	❏

The ultimate guide to mark making in the early years

Ensure that you model the use of your writing area for the children, e.g. sitting down at the desk and doing some writing (perhaps making notes to go in a child's learning journey/profile). By seeing you writing, and using writing to communicate meaning, your children learn that writing is of value and has a purpose.

Change the focus of your writing area regularly, to keep it fresh and exciting for the children. Use the children's interests to help you decide what focus to take. You could try:

An author's table: This works well for a focus on writing fiction or on a particular author. Take photos of the children in your class and laminate them, then offer these as character cards for your children to use in their stories.

An historical table: Use tea bags to stain paper for an aged feel. Offer the children scrolls of paper to write on, and feather quills and ink to write with.

A superhero table: Have a selection of superhero magazines and comics on offer. Laminate superhero cards, to give the children inspiration for characters to go into their writing. Make a superhero passport with details of the hero.

A Disney table: Have a selection of books with fairy tales and other Disney stories available. Laminate a set of Disney character pictures for the children to use in their story writing. A mirror works well for encouraging the children to put themselves into the story. Write on the mirror in dry wipe pen: 'Mirror, mirror, on the wall, who is the fairest of them all?'

You can use your writing area both for free writing and also for focused or adult-directed activities.

Making writing real

Think about times during your sessions or lessons when you need to use writing or make marks for a real purpose. Registration is a good example of this – you genuinely need to know who is in the session. Depending on their age and level of skill at writing, your children might:

- Make marks to self-register, for instance on a wipe-clean board.

- Write up their names on an interactive whiteboard.

- Slide their names onto the 'sad' or 'happy' columns on your interactive whiteboard.

- Stick laminated name strips with self fasteners to a felt board.

- Help you call out the names on the register, while you note who is present and absent.

Modelling writing

Find lots of ways to let your children see you using writing in real life situations. You might:

- Get the children to sit with you and comment/join in while you update their learning journeys or foundation stage profiles.

- Jot down observations about the children's play on sticky notes and ask the children to help you add these into their profiles.

- Sit with children to mark their writing, and to write positive comments and targets for improvement.

- Take 'orders' at snack time on an order pad.

- Model the use of writing frames on your interactive whiteboard to show the children how a particular form of writing works.

- Have a postbox in which you post messages to each other.

As you write, talk about the intellectual processes that are going on in your head. This use of metacognition (talking about our thinking) is very important in the development of higher order thinking.

Technology and mark making

The modern day world revolves around technology. Whereas just a couple of decades ago we had to communicate via letters and look up information in an encyclopaedia, now we can dash off a quick email or do a quick Internet search to find out the facts. The children we teach have been brought up with these new technologies – they are an integral part of their world, and something that has always been there for them. This means that technology can play a key part in showing your children that writing has a real purpose and value. You might use it to:

- Write a regular blog for parents, with your children contributing their ideas while you type them up.

- Create a website on which you feature samples of the children's writing.

- Make PowerPoints together with the children, to show their knowledge on a subject.

- Draw tracks or mazes for your Bee-Bots® or other remote control toys.

- Use online games to improve literacy. The BBC website is a great place for these.

- Watch an online animation of correct letter formation, or of how to make cursive joins.

- Model writing for and with your class on your interactive whiteboard.

Once children are writing, technology can offer a real lifeline to those who struggle, particularly those children who have issues with handwriting, who struggle with spelling or who have dyslexia. Voice recognition software offers the chance to communicate to those children with significant SEND that means they might never be able to handwrite.

activity

A TRIP TO THE SHOPS

You will need

- A large sheet of paper
- Marker pens
- A reason to visit the shops (see below)

Learning intentions

- To help the children understand that writing has a purpose
- To give an inspiration for mark making
- To link learning to a writing structure – the shopping list

Instructions

At preschool, one trip we have done with the children was to a local garden centre. Our preschool garden and allotment won the Alan Titchmarsh award from the Royal Horticultural Society (RHS). This meant we had an envelope full of vouchers to spend and a good reason to spend them. Before our trip, we wrote a shopping list with the children, with the adults modelling the writing process. We thought about what we needed to buy. We definitely wanted some high quality spades to use on our allotment.

Your trip to the shops might be for something simple, such as fruit and vegetables for snack time, or something unusual, such as a new animal for your school farm. You could look up information with the children about prices and shop opening times on the internet or in a local directory.

You can expand and extend this activity by writing shopping and other lists at different times of the year: a shopping list for Santa Claus, a packing list for going away on holiday in the summer, a list of questions for the children to ask the teacher they will have next year and so on.

Using provocations

A 'provocation' is a challenge or a puzzle, designed by the adults to get children thinking. The question 'how can we solve this?' is used to inspire the learning. As the children work together to answer the question, they talk, they extend their thinking, and they have a real and valid reason to make marks. The possibilities for different provocations are endless. Your provocation could be:

- A letter that the class receives from a storybook character who has a problem, e.g. the Prince in *Cinderella* saying he cannot find the princess who left her shoe behind.

- A situation that needs resolving, e.g. someone has been overfeeding the class pet and the children need to figure out who, and think up ways to stop this happening in future.

- An object or prop that has been left behind in the classroom, e.g. a handbag. How can we work out whose bag it is?

- A crime scene activity, e.g. the class toy has been stolen and some evidence has been left behind. How can we figure out whodunnit?

The ultimate guide to mark making in the early years

ANIMAL RESCUE

You will need

- Toy animals
- Bandages and sticky tape/masking tape
- Plasters
- Boxes of 'medication'
- A first aid kit
- Clipboards and pencils for the vets to take notes
- An old changing mat
- A baby bath or bowl with water in
- Cloths and sponges for wiping
- Some white 'vet' coats if available
- A diary and pencils/pens
- A telephone
- Boxes or animal containers/carriers
- Resources for the rescue: a rope, a stepladder, a net, etc.

Learning intentions

- To develop the children's fine motor skills
- To challenge the children to think outside the box
- To use a dramatic context as a basis for developing writing and thinking

Instructions

Set up an Animal Rescue Centre in your role play area – a place where injured animals can be brought to be treated. (The children may be familiar with the concept of animal rescue from watching television programmes such as *Dora the Explorer* and those featuring her cousin Diego, or from real life animal rescue documentaries on television.)

Have a variety of areas on offer within your Animal Rescue Centre: an area to clean and wash any injured animals; an area for treating them and bandaging injured limbs (great for fine motor skills); a reception area with a telephone and diary where you can take calls about injured animals, and note down the details when they are brought in; a surgery area, with clipboards for the vets to write their notes. You might also have a quiet area for the animals to rest in boxes, once they have been treated. The children can of course free play within their animal rescue centre, as well as trying to solve the provocation below.

The provocation

Set up a situation for the provocation ahead of time, by placing one of your toy animals in a tree or in a similar high up position. Have a variety of resources on hand for your animal rescuers to request: a rope, a step ladder. Make a phone call to your animal rescue team, from a passer-by who has seen the animal in trouble. Can they come and help with the rescue?

An extension

We tied our animal rescue theme in to a visit from a Rainforest Adventure group who showed the children a variety of exotic creatures such as a snake, a spider and a giant snail. We also had a visit from a group who brought in owls and other birds of prey to show the children, and for them to handle.

Writing in creative contexts

As well as writing for a real purpose, e.g. making a shopping list, writing can also take place in a real way within a creative context. Young children can enter a fictional world with ease, and this means you can offer them experiences, places and opportunities to treat as real that they might never have encountered outside the nursery or school environment. Creative contexts can be incredibly inspirational for children and are great for boosting self-confidence, for instance through performing to a small audience. You might be:

- Making marks to music, or to the sound of percussion instruments. How can we represent these sounds or beats using a pen or a paint brush? How can we show the lengths of the different sounds?

- Using dance to inspire mark making, e.g. children dancing on a large sheet of paper with paint on their feet.

- Acting out scenarios that involve writing, e.g. a parking attendant puts a parking ticket on the role play car or the prince writes some invitations to the Ball.

- Working together on an art project designed to communicate a message, e.g. a mosaic of your school motto or a new design or logo for your uniform.

At preschool, our children love the Yoga sessions, where we use stories and dramatised scenarios to encourage them to try out different Yoga moves. For instance using movements from the story of *The Very Hungry Caterpillar* (Eric Carle, Puffin, 2002) where the caterpillar comes out of the egg and eats the various foods.

'Real' role play environments

Your role play area offers a fantastic environment for purposeful mark making. You can relate the way you set up the area to a theme you are using in class, to the children's interests or to a particular skill or idea you want to introduce. It can be a good idea to talk with your children first about a new role play area. Your discussion might include talking about:

- What kind of things people might do in this setting.

- The kind of vocabulary that they might use.

- The kind of characters who might go here and what jobs or roles they would have.

- The sort of writing that might happen in this area.

- Whether the children have been to this type of setting in real life, and what their experiences of it were.

You can also model the use of a role play area for the children, with the help of another practitioner. For instance showing how the 'booking in' area at the garage could work, by modelling the conversation that a customer has when s/he brings in their car for repair. Use the list of environments and mark making/language activities below to inspire you:

- **Shoe shop:** boxes, shoes, shoe size chart and measuring ruler, order forms, receipts, tills.

- **Post office:** scales, phone, different sized envelopes, stampers, stationery, parcel wrapping with brown paper and tape, labels.

- **Garage:** tickets for car wash, office and reception area, booking in form, diary, calendar, car repair handbooks, telephones, role play vehicles, outdoor chalk for marking out 'bays', tools.

- **Restaurant:** cooking, weighing, writing recipes, ingredients, shopping, menus, order pads.

- **Airport:** x-ray machine to 'scan' cases, airline tickets, boarding passes, security area, lines of chairs to make the 'plane', suitcases, scales, labels, passports.

- **Garden centre:** plants, price tags, tools, tills, café area, catalogues, seed packets, planting demonstration.

- **Clothes shop:** clothes rail, mirror, price tags, hangers, changing rooms, tills, dressing up clothes, hats, bags, belts, shoes.

- **Hairdressers:** mirrors, scissors, model head with hair, diary, pictures of different hairstyles, magazines, till, telephones.

If you have space, it is useful to have a home corner on offer all the time with the usual kitchen items, sink, cooker, etc. Remember that a role play area can also be located outside, for instance a beach secenario in the summer months.

Deconstructed role play

In a deconstructed role play you offer the children a variety of multipurpose materials to use in role play as they wish. Rather than directing the play through the kind of role play area you have set up, the children use their imaginations. Your materials might include:

- Lots of large lengths of fabric

- Tarpaulins

- Pegs

- String and rope

- Cardboard boxes in all different sizes

- Sheets of flat cardboard/perspex

- Pipes, bricks

- Cardboard tubes and rolls

- Sticky tape, masking tape, parcel tape

Themes for writing

When making the decision about how and when to use themes and topics, consider how these can be linked to the children's interests and next steps. Themes can be particularly useful for writing because:

- They bring it to life, and give it a clear purpose.

- They are often inspired by, or lead on to, a trip somewhere outside of the school or nursery.

- They offer the children access to ideas, information and experiences that they might not otherwise access.

- They show how learning is linked – how the study of a theme links to skills and ideas in different areas of the curriculum.

- They often link to times of the year, e.g the seasons or festivals such as Diwali.

- They can be useful for inspiring fresh ideas for your teaching.

Rather than the full-length topics that used to be very popular but which failed to take account of children's interests, you might use mini themes to inform your planning in specific areas of learning. The children can initiate their own learning while you offer them access to fresh ideas and new experiences within continuous provision. Here are a few ideas for inspirational themes, along with suggestions about how they might lead to language learning and mark making across the curriculum:

Outer space: building a rocket (we used a giant cardboard box – wardrobe size from a storage company), silver foil, astronaut training school, countdown to take off, map of space, labels of the different planets, model of the solar system, star maps, going outside on a dark winter afternoon to look at the stars/moon, art using silver pens on a black background.

Fireworks Night: safety posters, scratch art of fireworks (colour the paper with stripes of different coloured crayons, then paint over with black paint and scratch out your fireworks), poems about firework noises, using percussion instruments to make a 'fireworks soundtrack'.

Under the Sea: a visit to an aquarium, making fact cards about different sea creatures, giant 'under the water' collage scene with labels, books such as Julia Donaldson's *Sharing a Shell*, films such as *Finding Nemo*, documentaries on different sea creatures.

The Great Fire of London: a trip to London to see the sights, 'fire' pictures using black silhouettes and red/yellow tissue paper flames, 3D pictures made inside a cardboard box, writing a diary entry about how the fire started, making a brainstorm together of words connected to fire.

As well as choosing a theme yourself to bring fresh learning to the children, you can also set up resources around a topic reflecting the children's current interests, for instance superheroes, dinosaurs or minibeasts.

Mark making in the outdoors

The outdoors offers a fantastic environment for mark making. Where possible, give children the chance to free flow between indoors and outdoors, for as much of the day as possible. The many positives of outdoor play, and mark making in the outdoors, include:

- There is much less pressure to keep tidy and clean.

- It is much easier to clean up (wash paint off the ground with a hose).

- The outdoors lends itself well to mucky and multisensory play.

- It is a multisensory environment in and of itself: the wind, the sun, the bird song (or the traffic noise).

- It encourages independence, for instance children putting on their coats by themselves before they come outside.

- The children can make choices about their play, and experiment with different materials (mud, sand, water, leaves, stones).

- For older children, it offers a break from the routine of the classroom, and a chance to let off steam.

In a free flow setting, children often choose to play outdoors rather than indoors. This means that it is essential to offer plenty of chances to make marks in your outdoor area. You might:

- Write letter shapes or numbers on the playground floor in chalk.

- Scribe in mud or sand, with a stick.

- Make a welcome mat just outside the door.

- Make notes on clipboards, e.g. taking measurements.

- Brainstorm words around a theme, with each theme contained in a circle (draw around the inside of a hula hoop).

- Mark 'bays' for your ride-on toys, and label the ride-on toys with a number. Number the bays and the toys and get the children to park them in the right place.

- Paint on long strips of lining paper (either pegged on a wall or laid flat on the ground).

- Go on a walk around the space and record what you see through photographs, drawings and recordings.

The practicalities

You are likely to be spending a lot of time outdoors with your children, particularly if they are able to free flow between indoors and outdoors. There are various practicalities to consider. For instance you may need to buy:

- High quality waterproof suits, which keep the children warm and dry whatever the weather.

- High vis jackets for the children and adults to wear when you go out on a walk or a trip.

- A cover for shade in the summer and to keep dry in the winter. If you have the funding, invest in a permanent covered area. We use a professional quality marquee because ours is a pack-away setting.

- A free flow curtain, made of PVC strips, to keep the heat indoors when the door to the outside is open.

- A storage rack for wellie boots.

Have plants growing in your outdoor area and incorporate an area for wildlife. You might look at your space and think this is not be possible, but it is surprising what you can achieve even in the smallest area. At our setting, we were given a tiny strip of disused land alongside the hall to make a garden. The ground was tarmac, so we had to use raised beds (you could use pots for a similar effect). We got parents and local businesses involved and created our garden with minimal financing. This is our build in progress:

And these are some pebbles that the children made marks on to go in the garden area: You can read the full story of our garden build on our website here: www.ourpreschool.org.uk/garden.html.

It's a great idea to create a portable grab-and-go writing toolkit for yourself, based on the kind of writing activities your children like to do outdoors. Your kit could include items such as mini clipboards, a pair of scissors, glue, sticky tape, pens and pencils, paper, envelopes, outdoor chalks, tape measures and compasses.

Part 8

From letters to words, from words to sentences

In this section

- Help children move from mark making to forming letters

- Support children to move from forming letters to writing words

- Build confidence in the early stages of writing

- Understand how spelling accuracy develops

- Support your children in developing clear handwriting

Consider this...

The final phase of learning to write involves teaching your children how to form and sound out letters and how to blend and segment words. This part of the process requires persistence, determination and repetition. It is not something that children will necessarily pick up through osmosis. It will need at least some adult-directed, adult-initiated and adult-supervised activities. In the year before they start in Reception, some children may be ready to start learning individual letter sounds. This will depend at least partly on their birth month. A child born in September will be 25 per cent older in terms of months than one born the following August, even though they will be in the same year group.

When children reach Reception year, the balance of activities tends to shift away from mainly child-initiated activities towards more of an emphasis on adult-directed learning. At this early stage of 'proper' reading and writing, reinforcement is key to success, whether this means reinforcing letter sounds, the correct way to form letter shapes or how to blend or segment words. Bad habits picked up at this age (poor pencil grip, incorrect letter formation) can stay with a child for life.

Reading, writing and talking are (or should be) very much equal partners in the process of becoming literate. Reading feeds into writing, and helps the child develop a wide and fluent vocabulary in written work. Phonics is very helpful in these early stages of reading and writing, especially for lower attaining children and for those who have not had access to lots of reading at home. Children's early writing tends to reflect their phonic knowledge. They will use the sounds they have learned in reading to write, sometimes with amusing results. If I see a word a hundred, a thousand, even a million times on a page when I'm reading, then I start to get comfortable with the shape, the look, even the feel of it when I spell it correctly. The current emphasis on systematic synthetic phonics makes this idea sound a bit like heresy but we cannot just spell words using sound, because different letter combinations can make the same sounds. Even as an adult, when I am writing and I come across a word I cannot remember how to spell, I rely as much on my knowledge of whether the word looks right as to how I might sound it out.

Interestingly, the same link between wide and avid reading applies to the acquisition of grammatical knowledge, and also to children finding their own writing voice. Yes, you can teach your children the naming of parts: what a subordinate clause looks like, how to spot and use a noun, a verb, an adjective or a connective. But if I read plenty of grammatically correct writing (and indeed hear grammatically correct English being spoken), I learn to use it in my own writing by seeing and hearing it modelled. Equally, if I hear the voices of thousands of different writers, I start to develop a feel for what works, and what kind of writing voice I would like for myself.

The structure of learning

As children move into the first year of statutory education, more time is spent on adult-directed literacy teaching than in the nursery/preschool years. In a Reception class in England there will typically be a focus on literacy and/or phonics each day, for around 20 minutes. There will also be focused small group activities supported by a teacher or teaching assistant, alongside plenty of child-initiated learning, perhaps around a topic or a theme. As the children move into Year 1, this time will lengthen to about an hour (what used to be called the Literacy Hour).

It is worth remembering that children of this age still have a short concentration span – typically, after 10 or 15 minutes they will benefit from a break or a change in the type of task. This is especially so for any summer born children. When you begin to introduce letters to a whole class, there are a number of important factors to ensure the most effective approach:

- Use a fast pace, so that the children stay engaged and focused.

- Move quickly through the learning, so that the children can almost immediately begin to form some words of their own.

- Incorporate lots of repetition. Find opportunities throughout the day/week to practise the sounds and to form the letters.

- Revise and refer back to what has gone before, incorporating it into child-initiated learning, as well as into adult-directed teaching.

- Keep the learning interactive, physical, practical, kinaesthetic. Make it really hands-on to 'stick' it in your children's minds.

- Use mnemonics and other memory tricks to help your children remember spellings.

- Pick apart and work with the language, talking about etymology and morphology right from the start.

- Get support from parents. Encourage them to revisit the day's learning at home to reinforce it, and so that you can move on quickly.

- Ensure that you maintain the children's confidence, especially for the lower attaining children.

- Keep an eye out for strugglers, get support in place for them as fast as possible.

- Watch out too for any children who are absent. Support these children in learning sounds that they have missed.

- Keep an eye out for your high attainers as well, and ensure that you stretch and challenge them, especially if they are already able to read.

From marks to letters: learning to read

There are approximately 44 phonemes in the English language (the exact number depends on the accent of the speaker). When you introduce the initial letter sounds to your children, model the actual sound for them rather than adding an 'uh' to the letter to make what we might describe as a 'letter sound'. So, the letter 's' is pronounced as 'sss' rather than as 'suh'. This will help them a great deal when it comes to blending the sounds together to make words ('sss – a – ttt' rather than 'suh – ah – tuh').

Learning letter/sound correspondences

The procedure for learning a letter/sound correspondence (or grapheme/phoneme correspondence) follows a similar pattern each time: the revisit/review, teach, practise, apply pattern, as described in the Letters and Sounds materials (see www.gov.uk/government/publications/letters-and-sounds). Of course, the teacher can make the various parts of the process as interesting, interactive, multisensory and resource-based as possible. The usual pattern is to:

- Introduce the letter to the group or class.

- Say the sound.

- Get the children to say the sound.

- Reinforce the learning through hands on, visual or other means (e.g. show the children the action that matches the sound as in the Jolly Phonics programme).

- Put the sound into context, that is identifying or demonstrating toys, objects, people, places, etc. with that sound in them.

- Play games or complete activities to reinforce the learning of the sound.

Structured phonics programmes

The majority of schools in England use some kind of systematic synthetic phonics (SSP) programme to teach literacy (Jolly Phonics, Read Write Inc, Letters and Sounds, etc.). Using a systematic programme has a number of benefits:

- It saves time and effort for the teacher in planning literacy.

- Often, the relevant resources are included (flash cards, worksheets, posters), again saving time.

- The structured nature of the programme means the phonemes are covered in a logical order.

- The teacher feels confident in offering the children a tried and tested method for learning to read.

- Schools have been match funded to buy these materials, thus saving costs for the setting.

- The lower attaining children, and those with SEND, may benefit from a highly structured approach.

However, there can be downsides to using a very structured programme. These programmes can, by their very nature be repetitive and creatively limited (particularly in the writing strands). They may also tempt you to hold back a high attaining child who just wants to get on with reading. Where you use a structured programme, take care that:

- You don't feel that you have to follow the programme slavishly, using all the materials, ideas and approaches provided, instead of considering what would work best for individual children.

- You give a context to the learning, remembering that words have a meaning as well as being a set of sounds, and that reading is about meaning, not simply about decoding what words say.

- You don't rule out other approaches, particularly for those children who struggle to read using phonics (for instance because of a hearing problem).

- You give plenty of support to the children in reading and spelling words that are irregular (often called tricky words).

- You introduce the children to a variety of ways of learning spellings, including those to do with whole word recognition and looking at the shapes of words.

- You maintain the joy of reading for your children, by sharing and working with plenty of stories and other texts as well as with reading scheme books.

- You offer plenty of chances for free writing, where getting meaning across is the aim, and not just writing tasks that involve repeated practice of a new sound.

Letter (and word) hunts

Children adore the idea of hunting for treasure. Capitalise on this by taking them on a letter or a word hunt. The children might:

- Hunt for letters hidden outside in a garden or in the school grounds, and use them to create words.

- Use a magnifying glass to find miniature words or letters hidden within your classroom.

- Find secret letters/words written in invisible ink, as though they are spies.

- Hunt for letters and words in different forms and formats: on cereal packets, on displays around the school, in story books or in comics.

- Bury a word that they don't like. I once heard a story about a teacher who got her class to do a funeral for the word 'nice' because she hated them using it so much. The person who told me said she had not been able to use the word 'nice' again since that day.

'LETTER OF THE DAY' or 'LETTER OF THE WEEK' AREA

YOU WILL NEED

- A set of letters (or single letter) on which you'd like to focus

- Lots of objects starting with those letters, or objects that have those sounds in them

- Plastic or magnetic letters and a magnetic board

- Laminated letter cards showing the correct formation

- Large examples of the letters, to display on your walls

LEARNING INTENTIONS

- To reinforce the children's learning of specific letters and sounds

- To match sounds with letters

- To make handwriting practice more engaging

- To link home and school to support literacy learning

INSTRUCTIONS

Create a 'Letter of the Day/Week' area within your classroom to help the children reinforce what they have learned in literacy. Incorporate plenty of resources and free choice activities within this area to reinforce the learning that has taken place in adult-directed sessions. For instance you could:

- Have a table with lots of resources on it that start with this letter or letters.

- Set the children the challenge of sorting objects according to the letter they start with.

- Ask the children to bring in something from home that starts with the letter.

- Have interactive games available on a laptop, for the children to play within the area.

- Create a treasure hunt where the children have to find examples of the letters hidden around your classroom, in an area outdoors, in the sand, in a feely bag by touch alone, and so on.

- Put a box of Lego® and a Lego® board in the area so that children can form letters and words out of the bricks.

From marks to letters: learning to write

Although reading and writing typically develop alongside each other during the first couple of years of school, writing is much harder for most children than reading. In order to be able to write, they have to:

- Work out what they want to say or talk about in their writing.

- Have the confidence to commit those ideas or thoughts to paper.

- Work out how to spell the words that they want to write down.

- Form the words on the page in a legible way.

A key aspect of this phase of the journey is the way that the teacher maintains each child's confidence and motivation to write. One useful way to do this is to give the child a framework to use, so that the structure and key words are already in place, and the child can then fill in the blanks, asking for words as needed. You can see an example of a framework here, used by a Reception age child to write a recipe for fruit kebabs.

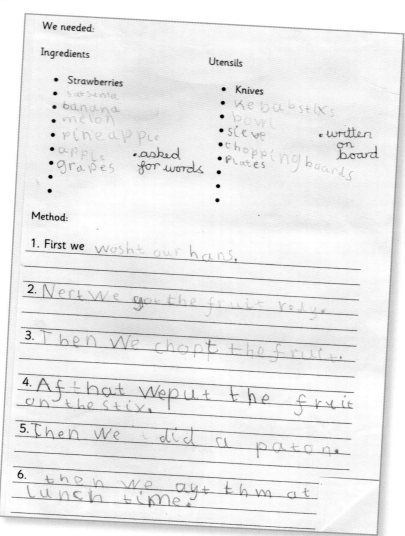

We needed:

Ingredients   Utensils

- Strawberries   - Knives
- satsuma   - kebabstixs
- banana   - bowl
- melon   - sieve   - written
- pineapple   - chopping boards   on board
- apple   - asked   - plates
- grapes   for words
-   -
-   -

Method:

1. First we washt our hans.

2. Nert we got the fruit redy.

3. Then we chopt the fruit.

4. Af that we put the fruit on the stix.

5. Then we did a paton.

6. then we ayt thm at lunch time.

Learning letter formation

When introducing the formation of individual letters, a similar pattern is usually taken to that which we use for teaching how to sound out phonemes:

1. Model how the letter is written to the whole class.

2. Get the children to use a movement-based approach to write the letter: write it in the air, write it on the back of the child in front of you, trace it on your palm.

3. Write the letter using a writing tool (on a mini whiteboard with a marker pen, on the interactive whiteboard).

4. Write the letter individually, using pencil on paper, reinforcing the learning through regular practice.

With Reception age children it can be a good idea to have lined handwriting books and ask the children to sit and do some individual handwriting practice when they come into your setting each morning. They could focus on practising the letter they learned the day before, for five minutes before registration each morning.

Teaching letter formation

Here are some useful ideas for teaching your children to form letters correctly, and encouraging them to practise the skills required while staying engaged and interested.

- Offer trace over cards, with a green arrow for the start point, and a red stop sign for the end point.

- Show how letters are formed on your interactive whiteboard (have an animation running over and over of the letters you are studying).

- Write the children's names on your interactive whiteboard, and get the children to trace over them. Gradually make them smaller, and when they are confident add surnames.

- Create laminated name cards for the children to use first thing in the morning to self-register. Ask them to trace over their name as accurately as possible then post it in your class postbox.

- Offer laminated letter mats, strips or cards which show the correct formation (and the joins in cursive writing). Supervise the use of these to ensure that the children learn correct letter formation.

- Get the children to be the teacher and correct your letter formation. Write a letter in the wrong way on the board. What did you do wrong and how can they correct you?

- Try this lovely rainbow letters activity. Offer the children a set of pencils matching the colours of the rainbow. They must trace over a letter with each colour of the rainbow in turn. By the time they do violet, the letter should have turned black!

You can find a link to a free set of downloadable letter formation cards on the companion website. (website)

The ultimate guide to mark making in the early years

From letters to words

As soon as the children have the first few sets of letters under their belts, they can start to blend and segment simple regular Consonant Vowel Consonant (CVC) words such as 'cat', 'dog' and 'tin'. To help support this process try splitting up words as you talk, during the course of your daily routine: 'Who knows where I've put my p – e – n?' or 'I want B – e – n to answer the next question.'

Get your children building banks of letters, phonemes and words to use in their writing. For instance you could:

- Have a bank of graphemes on your classroom wall, listed according to their connected sounds, which you regularly work through with the class. (Many of the structured reading programmes include a list of these for you to display.)

- Build a bank of words on a topic, to put in a topic display area. Write the words on laminated cards which you attach to the wall with self fasteners. The children can then borrow these to use in their writing.

- Brainstorm key vocabulary for a writing activity together on your interactive whiteboard, to act as a bank while they write.

- Have a bank of tricky words available on the wall for the children to take and use whenever they wish to write them – regularly used tricky words such as the, said, no, go, some, etc.

- Keep a small word book in which children record the words they use under the letters of the alphabet.

- Get your children to write out any words they find hard to spell three times in a bank at the back of a writing book.

- Create long lists of words, all using the same phoneme, or phonemes that follow the same pattern. This works well as a homework task, where the parents can support their child. For instance a list of words for: ar, er and ir; ch, sh and th; or u-e, oo and ew.

- Buy magnetic sets of words for your class to use whenever they need.

Learning tricky words

Over the centuries, the English language has borrowed many words from other languages and has been influenced by many other cultures. It has also evolved as a language, for instance where people started to pronounce a word differently, while still spelling it the same. Some of the key irregularities in English include:

- Words with a silent letter such as know and gnat.

- Words with the same letter combination such as ough but with a multitude of different pronunciations: thought, enough, through, though, bough.

- Words that are spelt differently, but which sound the same, such as: their and there (homophones).

- Words which are spelt the same, but pronounced differently, such as: 'wind up a clock' and 'wind' as in the weather (homonyms).

A key part of learning to write is to have strategies for those situations where a word cannot easily be spelt using phonic knowledge. This is why reading is so vital. Children internalise the spelling of irregular words that they see over and over again. Teach them how to remember spellings in a range of different ways:

- **By sight and shape**: examine the shape of the word. Which bits are high, which bits are low, does it have a flat or a bumpy shape? What does the overall shape look like?

- **By repetition**: get the tricky word into the child's memory by seeing or writing the word over and over again.

- **By focusing and thinking**: examine which bit of the word does not fit the regular pattern and work out a way to remember it, e.g. the word 'want' is pronounced 'wont', so tell your children to say it as 'want' with an emphasis on the 'a'.

- **By using a mnemonic**: the classic is 'big elephants can always understand small elephants' for spelling the word 'because'. Mnemonics are great for helping children remember how to spell regular combinations such as 'ould' – 'oh you little darling'.

- **By making connections**: many children find the spelling of the word 'said' tricky to remember, and will write it as 'siad' instead. If you talk about how the word 'said' is formed from the word 'say' it makes more sense.

- **By exploring the etymology**: 'one', 'once' and 'only' come from the same root, meaning a single unit of something.

- **By exploring the country or language of origin**: the word 'beautiful' has 'beau' from the French in it; the suffix 'psycho' comes from the Greek for 'mind'.

- **By adding a fun and physical element**: when teaching lists of homophones, get the children to 'kick the letter out of the way'. For instance to make 'sun' become 'son' they must 'kick the u out of the way'. Get them to stand up to kick it.

Teaching cursive handwriting

Depending on the policy at your school, children might start out with print, then move onto cursive (or joined up) handwriting at about age 6 or 7. Alternatively, you might be expected to start with cursive from the beginning. Often, it's a matter of habit, in that the teacher or school has always taught writing in a particular way. It's even a matter of nationality, with different countries taking different approaches. It's worth considering the points for and against teaching cursive from the start, rather than print. On the plus side with straight to cursive:

- Children don't have to learn a whole new writing style when they come to join up their letters.

- Cursive flows more easily across the page.

- Cursive writing can help the children develop a physical sense of how letters are formed.

- Because the letters flow from the left to the right, this tends to help children not mix up letters such as b and d.

- It is recommended by the British Dyslexia Association that children who have dyslexia write in a cursive style from the start.

On the downside with going straight to cursive:

- Most story books are written in print, so it is more intuitive for the children to read and write in this style.

- Most early years resources and posters use print, rather than cursive.

- Printing is easier for small hands, and the letters can be easily separated out.

- Cursive handwriting takes quite a bit of confidence, and some children might find it hard to form words at first.

- Cursive handwriting can look messy in early stages, as the movements are harder than those needed to print.

Overall, it's very much a matter of personal preference and habit. Some of the issues above can be overcome by teaching children their original print letters with entry strokes and exit strokes, so that they are ready to move onto joining up their letters when ready. There is no one correct order in which to teach the cursive strokes, although the movement required to join 'c' to 'c' is commonly taught first. You can find some useful links about cursive handwriting on the companion website. website

Teaching punctuation

In this age group, punctuation takes its very simplest forms. As you introduce each punctuation mark to your class, make sure that you help the children understand *what the punctuation mark does* as well as where it goes. What that means is, talk about the logic and purpose of a full stop or a capital letter within a piece of writing, as well as just telling them that it goes at the beginning or end of a sentence. Talk about the idea of one sentence containing a single set of ideas, and similarly about how commas can be used to separate a sequence of details within a sentence or to indicate a pause.

As with the teaching of reading and writing, ensure that you teach punctuation in a physical way. Get your children reading a sentence – stretching up to make the big capital letter at the start, and then 'punching out' a full stop to end it. Encourage them to take a breath before they begin to read the next sentence. You could describe this as 'sucking in some more super reading energy'. With commas, use a little 'hiccough' between each one to show how it feels to read a series of items on a list, as opposed to a longer pause between sentences after a full stop. Again, much of their knowledge about punctuation will develop as they become wide and avid readers.

Building writing confidence

There is often a lot of pressure on early years educators to push their children on with reading and writing. This pressure comes from all different directions: from parents, from local authority inspectors, from the Department for Education and often from the head teacher as well. However, children of course develop this skill at very different rates, and in many countries children are not even in school until they are six. Because literacy learning is often done in a whole class session, some children may struggle to keep up and to retain what has previously been learned. Where children start to lag behind, this can damage their confidence and put them off the very thing that you want them to feel happy about doing – writing! Make sure that you:

- Strike a balance between correcting bad habits (especially with letter formation) and correcting so much and so often that the child feels constantly under pressure to get it right.

- Use copying activities, particularly for those children who lack confidence. Write a word or sentence for the child to copy below (or have it available in print for them to copy).

- Use lots of fill in the blanks type activities using frameworks, where some or most of the sentence has already been written for the child.

- Use tracing activities to reinforce handwriting technique.

- Make sure you give plenty of time and opportunities for 'free writing' where the children can write what they want, without any pressure to spell correctly or to write neatly.

- Allow the children plenty of chances to use technology, so that they write via typing as well as via handwriting.

- Write as a whole class, with the children giving you their ideas and you scribing them on the board.

- Write via non written methods, for instance letting the children audio/video record their ideas, stories, etc.

- Offer the children sentence starters on laminated strips, to use in their writing.

- Teach techniques for getting ideas: brainstorming and mind mapping, the use of who, what, why, when, where and how.

- Offer the children writing frames and structures: the layout of a recipe form, the outline of a thank you card.

Copying writing

Where children need to build confidence in their writing or where they have a particular interest but not the vocabulary required to express it, copying activities can be very useful. In a way, copying from real life examples of writing is just as valid as copying from what the teacher has modelled on the board. In the example, the 6-year-old child has done an incredibly detailed piece of writing based on the Lego® Power Miners characters. This writing was self-initiated, with the child copying information from magazines and Lego® boxes and instructions to create a very detailed piece of writing.

Early grammar

As children begin to create longer sentences they will start to use features such as connectives and conjunctions. You can find a useful list for your young writers in the companion website. Again, talk to the children about the logic behind using connecting words – they join up two clauses or sentences to make a longer one. They can also show how events link together, how one event might cause another or the sequence in which events come. It can be tricky for children of this age to use connectives in a fluent way, to make longer sentences, while still making sense. Often they will use them to show a sequence of events, but within short sentences.

You can see this in the writing below, where the details of the trip to Westonbirt are given in sequence, but the sentences are still short and choppy. This piece of writing was an adult-directed activity done by a 5-year-old child.

Sentence in your head

When thinking about grammar and sentence construction, it is useful to encourage children to hold longer strings of words in their heads. As they get older, encourage your writers to form a whole sentence in their heads before they commit it to paper. This can be a struggle for children who have poor working memory, and it is worth practising it from the start. As soon as they are ready, encourage your children to answer questions in whole sentences.

It can sometimes take a while for children to form a word or sentence, or to finish what they are saying. Don't rush the child, or jump in before he has finished. Studies have shown that your children might need thirty seconds or so in order to form an answer. Show that you are interested and willing to wait. Demonstrate to the children that their ideas are important to you.

Supporting children who have dyslexia

Dyslexia is a learning difficulty which mainly affects a person's ability to read, write and spell. A child who has dyslexia will display a variety of symptoms, including the following:

- They attain well in some areas, but struggle particularly with reading, writing and spelling.

- They have difficulty sustaining attention and may appear to zone out.

- They have poor coordination and motor skills are generally slow to develop.

- Some attempts at spelling seem strange, and do not follow the phonic patterns that the class has learnt.

- The pencil grip is weak or poor, and the child finds it hard to stay close to the margin when starting a piece of writing.

- The child persistently confuses similar looking letters: b/d, p/g, m/w.

- There are lots of crossings out in writing and lots of attempts to spell a word in different ways.

- The child finds it hard to keep time properly and has poor personal organisation skills.

- The child has difficulty remembering sequences – days of the week, the alphabet.

If you suspect that a child has dyslexia, make sure that you refer them for a specialist assessment. The British Dyslexia Association (www.bdadyslexia.org.uk) is a great starting point for further reading.

A final word

I would like to wish you all the best with your mission to get your children mark making and enjoying writing. The act of written communication is one of the most wonderful gifts that we possess as human beings. It allows us to reach out to others, both now and in the future, through the marks that we make. To be there right at the start of the process means you play a vital role in your children's lives. I hope this book helps you encourage them, inspire them, support them and nurture them as they learn and develop. So good luck to you and all your children with the marks that you make!

Checklists and audits

The checklists and audit forms that follow are designed to get you reflecting on your setting and the way it is resourced and laid out. These forms should help you get the appropriate equipment and tools in place for mark making. They also act as a reminder of all those great ideas that float around within schools, books and across the internet.

 Visit the companion website for downloadable versions of all the checklists and audit forms.

Make marks with... checklist

We make marks with...	Tick
Chalk	❏
Felt pens	❏
Pencils	❏
Biros	❏
Large marker pens	❏
Dry wipe marker pens	❏
Charcoal	❏
Oil pastels	❏
Water colour pastels	❏
Paint brushes	❏
Tooth brushes	❏
Sponges	❏
Stampers	❏
String and wool	❏
Twigs, grasses and other natural materials	❏

Silver, gold and other metallic pens	❏
'Magic' water (water with glitter in it)	❏
Marbles	❏
Toys: cars, animals	❏
Our bodies: fingers, hands, toes, feet	❏
Food: fruit and vegetable prints	❏
Food: finger painting with chocolate	❏
Highlighter pens	❏
Stones (for making patterns)	❏
Coloured sands in shaker containers	❏
Play dough and clay letter sculptures	❏
Shaving brushes	❏
Watered down paint in water squirters	❏
Hole punchers	❏

Make marks on... checklist

We make marks on...	Tick
Diaries	❏
Calendars	❏
Sticky notes	❏
Birthday cards	❏
Mini individual whiteboards	❏
Large whiteboards	❏
An interactive whiteboard	❏
Full size clipboards	❏
Mini clipboards with pencils attached	❏
A1 size flipchart paper	❏
White paper	❏
Coloured paper	❏
Lined paper	❏
Squared paper	❏
Scrolls of paper	❏
Cardboard boxes	❏
Large flat sheets of cardboard	❏
Mini chalkboards	❏
Large chalkboard	❏
Outdoor walls	❏
Sheets of old/recycled wood	❏

Envelopes	❏
Postcards	❏
Long rolls of lining paper	❏
Rolls of wallpaper with different textured surfaces	❏
Clay	❏
Play dough	❏
Mirrors	❏
Stencils	❏
Paper taped under a table, as in a den	❏
Paper taped onto a table	❏
Sheets of foil (scratch with an old pen or stick)	❏
Etch A Sketch	❏
The ground outside	❏
The entrance to your setting (a 'doormat' in chalk)	❏
Shed walls	❏
A 'graffiti wall'	❏
Second hand or old and unused furniture	❏
Fences	❏
Sand	❏
Mud	❏
Laminated name cards for tracing over	❏

Space as a resource checklist

Our space has/is...	Tick
A dedicated 'Writing Area' for free choice or focused writing	❏
A dedicated 'Reading Area' with soft seating	❏
A quiet 'Listening Area' where children can focus	❏
Accessible resources children can use as/when they wish	❏
A mix of resources, regularly audited for relevance	❏
Interesting displays, at a level where the children can see them	❏
Open, uncluttered, easy for teacher/children to move around	❏
Areas divided off or partitioned from each other	❏
Welcoming to parents and children	❏
Displays in a variety of community languages, as appropriate	❏
Visual displays, signs and symbols	❏
Layout that allows for differentiated small group activities	❏
Comfy places for children to go to relax	❏
Displays to inform staff, as well as for the children	❏
Access to ICT for a variety of activities	❏

Space and communication audit

Where does most of the talking happen within our space?

Is most of the talking adult to child, child to child or adult to adult?

Where does most of the listening happen within our space?

Who does most listening – children or adults?

Are there any 'hot spots' where behaviour is a particular issue?

How many 'high impact' activities are there? (Ones that require close adult supervision or are particularly noisy or exciting.)

How do the children move around the space?

Do they follow the 'golden rules' when adults are not watching?

Displays audit

What do you first notice about the space?

What displays do you notice first?

What colours were first to catch your eye?

What colour or colours seem to predominate in the space?

Are you seeing mainly: children's work, adult's work or pre-printed materials?

Are the displays at a child's height or an adult's height?

Does the space feel cluttered or empty or just right?

If you could use one word to describe the displays, what would it be?

Glossary of words and abbreviations

Alliteration: the repeated use of initial consonant sounds.

Blending: running the letter sounds together to read a word, for example c – a – t makes cat.

Connective: a word that joins two sentences together, e.g. and, but, then.

Cursive writing: joined up handwriting.

CVC words: words with a consonant – vowel – consonant combination, e.g. cat, dog, dig, job.

Digraph: two letters (a grapheme) that represent a single sound: the 'ai' sound in rain and Spain, or the 'ng' sound in king and sing.

EYFS: the Early Years Foundation Stage, the phase from birth to five years old for early years practitioners working in England.

Grapheme: a way of writing down a phoneme.

Homophone: words that are spelt differently, but which sound the same, such as 'son' and 'sun' and 'you' and 'ewe'.

Metaphor: a figure of speech in which the writer uses an item, image, story, etc. to represent something else, for instance 'Her life was an open book'. Unlike a simile, a metaphor does not use 'like' or 'as', but says that one thing is another.

Phoneme: the smallest unit of sound in a language that can convey meaning. This could be a single letter (the 's' sound in sing), but it can also be more than one letter (the 'f' sound made by the 'ph' in phoneme).

Prosody: the 'music' of speech – putting our emotions over through the sound of our voices (see also 'tone').

Segmenting: splitting a word up into its individual sounds (phonemes) to spell and write it, e.g. the word cat segments into c – a – t.

SEND: Special Educational Needs and Disabilities. A child who has 'SEND' needs some kind of adaptation to best access learning.

Symbol: an image (either written or visual) which stands for something else, e.g. the golden 'M' at McDonalds. In writing, a tree struck by lightning might symbolise the break up of a relationship (this is also known as 'pathetic fallacy').

Syntax: the way that a sentence is constructed.

Tone (of voice): using the sound of your voice to express an emotional feeling (either real or pretend). For instance, sounding disappointed if a child misbehaves, or excited to introduce a new activity.

Trigraph: three letters (a grapheme) that when written down represent a single sound – the 'igh' sound in high and sigh.

Vocabulary: the number of words of a language that a person knows as in, 'he has a wide vocabulary'.